It's as Plain as Black and White

It's as Plain as Black and White

**HOW RACE AND RACISM SHAPED
AND MOTIVATED ME**

By

C. E. Dickens

ISBN: 9798647153760 (paperback)

Disclaimer
This is a work of creative non-fiction. All of the events in this memoir are true to the best of the author's memory. Some names and identifying features have been changed or omitted to protect the identity of certain parties. The author in no way represents any company, corporation, or brand mentioned herein. The views expressed in this memoir are solely those of the author.

Dedication

—ɯ—

This book is dedicated to all who have endured before me. To those who made a positive contribution in my life and endured before the playing field became level and equal, by law. Many of the names will remain anonymous to the world, but to those who were trailblazers, you will forever remain near and dear to my heart and spirit.

In loving memory of my brother-in-law Robert, a.k.a. R. B. A husband, father, easygoing and diligent worker, and servant leader who spent his entire life tending to the needs of others. Not only did he care for the needs of others, but he also loved animals. As a result of his affection for animals, he spent a large percentage of his life caring for them. In retrospect, he may have been more comfortable around the animals he loved and cared for rather than people who were often critical and insensitive to perceived physical imperfections. The revelations revealed in this book are symbolic of his struggles to be respected and understood.

In loving memory of my sister-in-law Trina, an artist. She is credited with creating the original artwork shown on the cover of this publication. Admittedly, like her, this artwork is truly loved and admired by me. But more than that, my sister-in-law was one of the most *it's either black or white* persons I have ever known. True, real, raw—no matter the consequences. In keeping with the *It's As Plain As Black and White* theme, it is only fitting that her spirit and influence are reflected throughout this literary piece of work.

And to my yet-to-be-born grandchildren. I cannot imagine what the world will be like upon your arrival. But one thing I do know is that it is necessary for each of you to know and understand the challenges of those who sacrificed and paved a path for you to excel and succeed. Since others may not adequately share this story, I have chosen to share this story in my own words and on my own terms. My heartfelt feelings are that no matter how factual others may attempt to be, no one can truly tell this story for me, other than me. My hope is that you will gain insight and an appreciation for understanding the struggles of those who came before you. My challenge to each of you is that you will take the baton and continue to run this race stronger, faster, and further than those who came before you. Finish what others have started—run through the tape.

> *We hold these truths to be self-evident: that all men are created equal; that they are endowed by their Creator with certain unalienable rights; that among these are life, liberty, and the pursuit of happiness.*
> —Thomas Jefferson

Table of Contents

—⚍—

Foreword

—ᗰ—

Racism. Just the word by itself elicits feelings of strong emotions that reside in the depth of all of us. So the question that has long plagued this country, plagued the world, is how do we as a society have a civil conversation about a topic that brings forth such great emotion from within?

C. E. Dickens has found a simplistic but profound way to discuss the topic of racism. In his book, *It's As Plain As Black and White*, the author approaches the very controversial topic by disarming his readers and sharing an intimate portrayal of his story of how racism has influenced his life, hindered it, and even helped him achieve peaks that it was originally designed to stop. Once you start reading this account, you will be hard-pressed to put it down. It doesn't even feel like you are reading a book but rather having an intimate conversation over a cup of coffee with an old friend.

I have read many accounts on and about racism. Most are emotionally charged with a rawness that can't be overlooked and often leave the reader emotionally drained. When most think about racism in this country, our mind immediately goes to black vs. white. Mr. Dickens approaches the subject from a fact-based, academic perspective with credible sources, statistics, quoted data, and his personal story. He uses his experiences but frames them in such a manner that it speaks to us from a purely human perspective. In turn, this disarms the reader from personal perspectives to more of a global perspective, which we can all relate and understand, to some point.

It's As Plain As Black and White does not try to answer the question of how we resolve the issue of racism, but it does hold a mirror up to the face of every individual who reads it. I found myself examining my personal thoughts, experiences, and feelings about racism.

Now, most forewords are written only as an introduction to encourage the reader to read it; however, I was so intrigued by this book, I added one simple thought of my own. For that, I do ask your forgiveness for this not being the typical foreword, but then this isn't the typical book either.

In my conclusion, I have surrendered to the belief that racism will exist as long as mankind exists, and as long as racism exists, then so will prejudice. The real test for mankind, as C. E. Dickens eludes to, is to not let our own beliefs, personal opinions, or thoughts be the sole judge of a person or group of people. We must base our judgments on facts and facts alone. If we can do this as individuals, then as a society racism will die, and if there is no racism, then prejudice will cease to exist as well. Only then can we truly declare that we have become an evolved civilization and that we operate in a world where racism does not truly exist.

Warning: The book you are about to read, *It's As Plain as Black and White*, is written in one of the purest and rawest forms that I have ever read for a non-fictional piece. The topic of racism in the United States is deeply explored and discussed through the author's own eyes and experiences.

I caution you that this work will elicit deep feelings and emotions regardless of race, gender, age, education, and social-economic standing. I would encourage all readers to brace their minds, emotions, and any preconceived ideas that they may have about racism in this country and the effects that it has on those who are subjected to it.

I hope you enjoy *It's As Plain As Black and White* as much as I have.

—Homer L. Randle III

Introduction

—⁊⁊⁊—

Racism and race are two of the most controversial issues of our time. Not only are these two topics controversial, but they are also very impactful to today's society as well as our future, affecting the greater good and impacting all. Oftentimes, those of us who are impacted the most are often the ones who are the least likely to publicly speak out. Many may feel the platform for speaking out against racism is limited, not worth the backlash you may endure, or even intimidating. My goal is to be a voice for the voiceless by sharing my experiences for the purpose of acknowledging the negative, increasing awareness, and trying to accentuate what was learned from the devastating practice and impact of racial bias and racism. This very complex issue can be solved or minimized through open and direct dialogue, understanding, education, a willingness to change past faults, and an acknowledgment of history and its supporting facts.

As a member of the baby boomer generation, I have been afforded a very unique vantage point to experience and observe the evolving racial climate of our time. Some Jim Crowe laws—anti-civil rights laws—were still front and center during the '60s, and various types of protests were the bedrock of the '70s. During the '80s, the Supreme Court found that sexual harassment is a form of illegal job discrimination. In the '90s, the gap narrowed between equality for men and women, and the election of Barack Obama shocked us after the turn of the century. Finally, in the present-day political climate, there are racial and class divisions and a reversal of previous hard-fought social, economic, racial, legal, criminal justice, and employment gains. The progress achieved during the last fifty years appears to be crumbling right before our very eyes in the present-day political climate.

Is it possible to be passionate about and raise the issue of race and racism without being labeled radical? If it is not possible, then this is a risk I am willing to take.

Many of us find comfort in operating where there is a gray area. In fact, when contemplating choices and situations, for some, operating in a so-called gray area is welcomed and expected. Gray areas imply could be, maybe, I don't know, I'm not sure, and it's possible type of responses or reactions to ill-defined situations not conforming to clear-cut clarity or what is undeniable or obvious. Some degree of latitude or give-and-take is expected when operating within a gray area.

In contrast, using the phrase "it's either black or white" implies straightforwardness, something that is clearly identifiable, concise, or void of doubt. The *maybe*, the *if*, or the *I'm not sure* is minimized or eliminated. Saying something is either black or white is the opposite of operating within a so-called gray area. Oftentimes, viewing something as either black or white is viewed by others as being inflexible, resistant, and rigid. Depending upon the environment you may find yourself in, viewing something as either black or white can be labeled as a negative. But in the case of this book, the intended purpose is to promote what is real, relevant, undeniable, and verifiable.

Routinely, we encounter several different definitions of race and racism. To be clear, within the context of this publication, race is defined as the idea that the human species is divided into distinct groups based on inherited physical and behavioral differences. However, racism is defined as prejudice, discrimination, or antagonism directed against someone of a different race based on the belief that one's own race is superior.

As those of my generation live their lives and mature, our life experiences and longevity tend to propel us more toward openness and the likelihood of taking on challenges that otherwise many may avoid. In contrast, younger generations may not necessarily display the same level of patience and thoughtfulness with current-day racial issues.

As I have grown, I am driven and motivated by truth and reality. Truth and reality are motivators for my decision to create and publish *It's As Plain As Black and White: How Race and Racism Shaped and Motivated Me*.

I believe race and racism can be viewed as black and white. *It's As Plain As Black and White: How Race and Racism Shaped and Motivated Me* is my personal perspective of how I encountered various levels and elements of racism. It occurred to me that just as the title reveals a raw, straightforward approach to a topic many would like to avoid, race and racism are front and center in our everyday lives whether we acknowledge it or not. Our failure to acknowledge the impact of race and racism does not permit this issue to be quietly and discreetly removed to the background of society. As a result of my life's experiences and my pursuit of championing a level playing field for all, I have grown to value the opportunity to reflect and speak out on the complex issues of race and racism.

Every person, regardless of race, creed, or color, deserves to be treated with dignity, fairness, equality, and respect. Anything less is inhumane, uncivil, and a violation of the basic rights as reflected in the constitutional amendments and major civil rights acts of Congress.

In writing this book, my goal is to help create a dialogue about racism by sharing how race and racism impacted me and shaped my outlook on life. My purpose for writing about racism involves sharing some of my personal and professional experiences while attempting to illustrate how those experiences positively impacted my life. Yes, I did say positively. You see, throughout my life, I have refused to allow the actions of others to negatively shape me.

Why does racism even exist? Racism is a deep-rooted issue. I would suggest that causes and solutions to the problem are very complex. Depending upon who is doing the speaking, the causes and solutions can be approached from a social science, political, or biblical viewpoint. Today, I am not focused on attempting to create a solution to racism; perhaps only the Creator can create a solution to this massive and complex problem that plagues all of humanity. No matter the risk and as difficult and painful as the topic of racism may appear, it is something that I am driven to talk about. I am continuously in awe of racism and its cause and effect on the lives of those who practice it and those who are impacted by it. I have often wondered why someone would want to judge and practice bias against another simply based on the color of someone's skin or their ethnicity, religious belief, or culture. What is it about another person's skin color that would make someone want to hate and discriminate?

This book is not written for the purpose of reaching the masses. This is why I did not formally ask colleagues to offer preview comments or endorsements. I am fully aware that many folk—people of color as well as Anglo-Americans—will be very skeptical about this book and this topic. Each side will be skeptical for different reasons. I believe that there is a percentage of African Americans who feel as if they have achieved the American dream as a result of their hard work and sacrifice. Therefore, why can't the rest of the people within their culture do the same? Their thinking is, maybe we should just shut up and try harder. Typically, people who fit into this category try so hard for acceptance, but soon discover it's just a matter of time before they encounter a situation that reminds them of exactly how they are viewed by many who are outside of their race. No amount of money, power, or status will change the color of your skin. On the other hand, there are some Anglo-Americans who deny that double standards, white privilege, racial preferences, and even racism exist. These are the same people who always wonder why we have to always talk about race or play the *race card*. These are the same people who somehow find justification in talking about reverse discrimination or the angry white male. I don't know about the so-called race card, but I will tell you that racism, discrimination, and racial injustice are real—very real. Not only that, when you have grown up your entire life living on the peripheral of the bottom rung of society, your psychic radar operates differently when confronted with perceived biases.

We could conduct a hypothetical survey and ask the questions: How many blacks wish they were born white? How many whites wish they were born black? What do you think the outcome of this survey would be? If people of color don't run Wall Street, own any Fortune 500 companies, don't control major media outlets, don't control the armed forces, don't oversee the top-rated institutions of higher learning, and are not the majority in local, state, or national politics, then why in the world is there so much fear and anger toward people of color?

This book is written in part for future generations. The future of our society will rest with this progressive-thinking and highly educated group. Everyone must understand that when you encounter everyday life and engage others in work or leisure, you must be fully prepared to counteract bigotry and racism, whether it is anticipated or unanticipated. This is the case because you will most certainly encounter a diverse group of individuals who may have different motives, viewpoints, beliefs, and morals. If you are not prepared, and if you do not recognize what is happening around you and to you, you will suffer uncompromising challenges while in pursuit of life, liberty, justice, and equality. Recognizing, understanding, and developing a personal resolve in overcoming racism is a key to your personal and professional survival.

If you could, for a day, take those who are members of the majority and place them in a situation where they were suddenly the minority, I believe their points of view would change dramatically. Don't be too quick to judge another man until you have had the opportunity to walk in his shoes.

I want to share some of my experiences. Perhaps my experiences will provide some insight, hope, inspiration, motivation, and encouragement to someone who may have felt that what they were experiencing was an isolated situation. If true, let me assure you that your encounters with racism are by no means isolated. Others who may struggle with this issue reside on an island with you that is more populated than you may realize.

As the author, *It's As Plain As Black and White: How Race and Racism Shaped and Motivated Me* symbolizes an unveiled spirit of liberation. Deep within each of us lies an indomitable human spirit. Sometimes this spirit can remain dormant while there are other times when that same dormant spirit can explode like a volcano. Whether seen or unseen, the power of the human spirit in the human species is always lurking, waiting to be unleashed for the purposefulness and usefulness of its owner.

Let's be clear about one thing: each of us (all) have some type of bias and/or prejudice. I do not believe we are born with these prejudices; somewhere along the way, we are taught certain biases and prejudices, or they were simply learned. We are human; we have vulnerabilities. I cringe whenever I hear anyone say, "I don't have a prejudice bone in my body." Educated, open minded, moral conscious-inspired, integrity-inspired, and ethical people understand the cancerous impact of exerting biases and prejudices against others. There is even bias within cultures. Sadly, I have been a recipient and a witness to this type of bias. Each person should seek to understand how harboring any form of bias can impact others. Empathy is often the key.

Very often we are our own worst enemy as we foolishly build stumbling blocks on the path that leads to success and happiness.

—Unknown

Note: The words African American, black, Black American, Negro (noted quotes), white, Caucasian, Anglo American, Hispanic, Latino, Natives, Native Americans, Asian, Asian American, people of color, and minorities are used interchangeably throughout this book.

How Race and Racism Shaped and Motivated Me

—ᴍ—

These photographs were retrieved from the annals of the civil rights movement. They represent the struggle for justice and equality. Progress was achieved as a result of the sacrifices, the human spirit, and the resolve demonstrated by brave protesters who realized the movement was much greater than any one individual. Those of us who benefitted or were impacted by the actions of these courageous people owe a great debt and gratitude. We are duty-bound to accept the baton that has been passed to us as we run our designated leg of the race for justice and equality.

—⋙—

Justitia, circa 1 AD, is the Roman goddess of justice. The scales represent judgement and fairness, the blindfold represents impartiality, and the sword represents punishment/law. This gives all quite a good précis of justice symbols, both modern and historical derivatives. For clarity, précis is a concise summary of essential points, statements, or facts.

CHAPTER 1

Where My Journey Began— Setting the Scene

—⚬—

You grow up and recognize that in an educated, secular society,
there's no excuse for ignorance. You have to recognize in yourself,
and challenge yourself, that if you see racism or homophobia or
misogyny in a secular society, as a member of that society, you
should challenge it. You owe it to the betterment of society.
—Hozier

—⚬—

BEFORE I CAN BEGIN TO fully explore *It's As Plain As Black and White: How Race and Racism Shaped and Motivated Me*, it is important for me to share initial insight on the who, what, when, where, and how of what shaped and influenced me. To fully understand my foundation and personal platform, it is necessary to start this journey from its core: my birthplace and early youthful circumstances.

As a youth growing up in a small town in the Florida Panhandle, I was a *dreamer*, but my dreams did not permit me to truly fathom or comprehend where I am today, celebrating the benefits of hard work and good decision-making resulting in achievement. You see, as the product of a single-parent household, I could have easily become a statistic; however, God had more in store for me than I could have ever imagined. Not only that, God uniquely and divinely placed powerful and positive role models in my life who acted as a beacon along the rocky shoreline to help guide me and show me the way.

Early in my life, I am not exactly sure when, I recognized and developed a strong concern for mankind and a thirst for equality. I am not sure if this attribute was developed as a result of my upbringing, the work ethics that were modeled by my mother, my education, or a combination of several if not all contributing elements.

My strong concern for mankind and a preference for equality profoundly motivated me. Later, pursuing excellence was instilled in me as a result of my military service. Combined, these attributes set me on a path that became my foundation for surviving on a personal as well as a professional level. In my mind and in my heart, I truly believed that whatever others could achieve, I could achieve as well. I believed whatever lifestyle others may have had, I could live that same lifestyle. But not only that, I believed I could exceed whatever standards were established. Each phase of my life was predicated on these beliefs.

In 1927, what is believed by many as the last spectacle lynching in the United States—the lynching of Claude Neal—occurred in Jackson County, Florida. After the lynching, Claude's mutilated body was transported and hung on a tree on the northeast corner of the courthouse square, the Plaza. I will not delve further into the ugly and horrific facts surrounding this incident except to say it is a part of a well-documented and recorded history. Amazingly, after growing up in this area, I was not aware of the history of this event until many years later, after I had left the area and become an adult. For whatever reason, I do not recall anyone, black or white, speaking of this historical and horrific incident during my upbringing. There was no mention of this incident in the public school system. For further historical insight about this time and region, please refer to appendix two.

When most think of Florida, they think of white sandy beaches, aqua-blue water, tourism, NASA, and Disney; however, there is another Florida commonly called the Panhandle. Even though the Panhandle is Florida, the lifestyle of this area resembles that of South Alabama more so than the typical images of Florida. In fact, I grew up less than forty miles from the Florida-Alabama state line. Hurricane Michael ravaged this area during the fall of 2018.

As an overview, the residents of this area are very conservative and deeply committed to their faith. This area is known for fishing, hunting, and agriculture. According to the census of 2000, there were 6,230 people, 2,398 households, and 1,395 families residing in my hometown. The racial makeup was 56.8 percent white, 40.2 percent African American, 0.3 percent Native American, 0.7 percent Asian, 0.9 percent from other races, and 1.1 percent from two or more races. Hispanic or Latino of any race were 2.6 percent of the population.

The median income for a household was $23,861, and the median income for a family was $29,590. Males had a median income of $28,500, versus $21,530 for females. The per capita income was $14,021. About 20.9 percent of families and 28.5 percent of the population were below the poverty line, including 41.7 percent of those under age eighteen and 34.6 percent of those age sixty-five or over.

There were 2,398 households, of which 28.8 percent had children under the age of eighteen living with them, 34.3 percent were married couples living together, 20.7 percent had a female householder with no husband present, and 41.8 percent were nonfamilies. Thirty-eight percent of all households were made up of individuals, and 19.3 percent had someone living alone who was sixty-five years of age or older. The average household size was 2.22, and the average family size was 2.96.

From 2014 to 2015, employment in the county declined at a rate of -0.8 percent, from 15,747 employees to 15,621 employees. The most common employment sectors for those who lived in the county are healthcare and social assistance, retail trade, and public administration.

Considering the number of people who live in or below the poverty level, it amazes me how America can spend billions of dollars on our military and foreign aid, yet we have these bitter fights among ourselves about providing government assistance for those who are genuinely in need.

Prior to Hurricane Michael, antebellum homes dominated the landscape, and eco-tourism was a burgeoning business. Thanks to an abundance of natural beauty, miles of spring-fed rivers, lakes, and ponds, paddling trails that draw kayak, canoe, and paddleboard enthusiasts to explore the local waterways, many considered this area as an outdoor paradise. As a child growing up in this environment, I spent countless hours roaming through the woods, dreaming and exploring.

What did I learn from this experience?

When you began life at the so-called bottom, you do not become unglued when you encounter the challenges of everyday life. One's personal experiences, while also observing others as they endure hardships, can be an enormous motivator if channeled properly. The work ethics, commitment, sense of accountability, and responsibility that I experienced were huge foundation builders for my life. Humbleness, integrity, and respect for others in today's society are diminishing personal attributes. These are the types of attributes that were instilled in family members with small town, rural values. A sense of family and neighbors pitching in to help neighbors was prevalent throughout the community. The values and beliefs that were instilled in me helped me throughout my personal and professional life.

Oftentimes, poor neighborhoods are confronted with very serious community enhancement and environmental challenges as well as issues involving neglect. After living in, observing, and understanding how poverty can impact you, I developed a watchful eye for understanding and raising my conscious level for attention to detail. As examples, when buying a home or car, signing a contract, or indulging in any other major investment, pay attention to the details so that others will not be in a position to take advantage of you. Research is critical. Failure to properly research could result in dealing with potential problems that you did not foresee.

Once I expanded my territory through travel and acquired a view of how the rest of the world functioned, I was always drawn back to the place of my birth. The reflection caused me to dream. This reflection motivated me. This newfound view made me realize that whatever others could achieve, I could achieve also. But not only could I do it, I could do it and excel at it as well.

Because of my upbringing, I was raised not to hate or practice bias against anyone. As with most of us, I have seen and witnessed my fair share of racial injustice, having the right temperament of knowing when versus when not to react is key. In fact, I believe the decision to react or not to react is a learned skill. I can credit my upbringing with having the ability to remain calm in the midst of fighting off the desires of (sometimes) wanting to strike back or retaliate.

It's not about where you are from; it's about the journey and where you are going. It's about the values, morals, and beliefs that were instilled in you. It's not about how rich or poor you are; it's about getting along with others and understanding the meaning of life. It's about helping others. It's about leaving this world a better place than the world you inherited.

I would suppose that someone else who may have grown up in the same or similar surroundings as I did and who was of a different ethnicity could conceivably share a totally different experience. This is what is so unique about individual experiences; they are expressed from the viewpoint of each individual person. What is viewed as racism and injustice is in the eye of the beholder. I am convinced that the black-versus-white experience in America provides a stark contrast into how life in general is viewed. In fact, the Kerner Commission and the data provided by the Pew Research Center mentioned later in this book supports this assertion. We hear the rhetoric about equality, but do we see the facts? Fair application of the law, truth, facts, and evidence should prevail in situations where varying points of view are brought into question. Oftentimes, even the law, truth, facts, and evidence are skewed to produce outcomes that may enhance personal and political preferences.

I am proud of my humble beginnings. I cherished my time growing up in the rural Florida Panhandle. It provided me with the necessary foundation that fueled me to do and want more out of life. If I had the opportunity to change this portion of my life, I would politely decline. Everybody has a story; this is what makes each person so unique.

How was I shaped and motivated by chapter one?
Each human being is unique. The different environments that reflect where our journeys began are just as diverse and unique as we are individually. We are shaped by many different factors, including how we were raised as well as our values, morals, beliefs, social-economic backgrounds, education, and so much more. Sometimes this impact can be positive while at other times our environments can create viewpoints that produce an unhealthy outlook toward others.

Oftentimes, it is difficult to share or express your heartfelt opinions without some degree of transparency. Some elements of transparency promote insightfulness to others, emphasizing why we feel what we feel or why we think the way we think. While attempting to connect with others, your experiences are vital to the connection process.

Our differences should not be a liability but an asset. Our differences should not prohibit us from finding a common ground. A common ground is sharing a desire for respect, equality, and human decency for all mankind. Where it all began for me is the panhandle of Florida, but where or when it will all end is unknown. This is how and why I am impacted by chapter one, Where My Journey Began—Setting the Scene.

> *A people without the knowledge of their past history, origin, and culture is like a tree without roots.*
>
> —Marcus Garvey

CHAPTER 2

Black and White— Let's Go Deeper

—⚊—

Racism comes in many different forms. Sometimes it's subtle, and sometimes it's overt. Sometimes it's violent, and sometimes it's harmless, but it is definitely here. It's something I think we all are guilty of, and we just have to make sure that we deal with our own personal racism in the right way.
—Jordan Peele

—⚊—

I AM REMINDED OF THE many stereotypical symbols and meanings connected with describing black versus white. Where did these stereotypical symbols and meanings come from? Who created them and why? I do not know the origin of these symbols and meanings, but I can certainly acknowledge they have underlining meanings and have been around as long as I can remember. Let's examine a few of these well-known symbols and meanings.

Black Symbolisms
The black color is the absence of color. Black is a mysterious color that is typically associated with the unknown or the negative. The color black represents strength, seriousness, power, and authority. Black is a formal, elegant, and prestigious color.

7

Authoritative and powerful, the color black can evoke strong emotions, and too much black can be overwhelming.

In heraldry, black is the symbol of grief. The color black can be serious, professional, and conventional, but black can also represent mysterious, sexy, and sophisticated. Black is a visually slimming color for clothing, and like other dark colors in interior design, black can make a room appear to shrink in size.

The color black affects the mind and body by helping to create an inconspicuous feeling, boosting confidence in appearance, increasing the sense of potential and possibility, or producing feelings of emptiness, gloom, or sadness.

In Western countries black is the color of mourning, death, and sadness. Black often represents the emotions and actions of rebellion in teenagers and youth. The color black can represent both the positive and the negative. As the opposite of white, movies, books, print media, and television typically depict the good guy in white and the bad guy in black. In more recent times, the good guy is shown in black to create mystery around the character's identity.

Other meanings associated with the color black include the following:

- The term *black tie* refers to a formal event or dress code.
- The description *pitch-black* references no light or no visibility.
- The term *black-hearted* describes an evil person.
- A *black belt* is an expert level in martial arts.
- The term *blackwash* is to bring things out in the open.
- The phrase *in the black* refers to having money or profiting and doing well in business.
- A *black box* is a piece of equipment or apparatus usually used in airplanes.
- A *black eye* is damage to an eye, including bruising and discoloration, or damage to one's reputation.
- A *black sheep* is an outcast from a family or from society.
- The phrase *men in black* refers to government agents.
- A *blacklist* is a list of people or organizations to boycott, avoid, or punish.
- The term *blackguard* is used to reference a bad guy or a scoundrel.
- The word *blackmail* refers to obtaining something by threat.
- The word *blackout* means a loss of electricity, loss of visibility, turning

out the lights, loss of consciousness, or the act of erasing or deleting something.
- The term *black market* refers to the illegal trade of goods or money.

White Symbolisms

White, an inherently positive color, is associated with purity, virginity, innocence, light, goodness, heaven, safety, brilliance, illumination, understanding, cleanliness, faith, beginnings, sterility, spirituality, possibility, humility, sincerity, protection, softness, and perfection.

The color white can represent a successful beginning. In heraldry, white depicts faith and purity. As the opposite of black, movies, books, print media, and television typically depict the good guy in white and the bad guy in black.

The color of snow, white is often used to represent coolness and simplicity. White's association with cleanliness and sterility is often seen in hospitals, medical centers, and laboratories to communicate safety. The color white is also associated with low-fat foods and dairy products.

To the human eye, white is a bright and brilliant color that can cause headaches. In cases of extremely bright light, the color white can even be blinding.

Throughout the Western countries, white is the traditional color worn by brides to signify purity, innocence, and virginity. In Eastern countries, the color white is the color of mourning and funerals. In certain cultures, white is the color of royalty or of religious figures, as angels are typically depicted as wearing white or having a white glow. A white picket fence surrounds a safe and happy home.

The color white affects the mind and body by aiding in mental clarity, promoting feelings of fresh beginnings and renewal, assisting in cleansing, clearing obstacles and clutter, and encouraging the purification of thoughts and actions.

White gemstones are believed to help create new beginnings, remove prejudice and preconceived notions, to see the innocence in others, and to clear emotional clutter and silence the inner critic.

Other meanings associated with the color white include the following:

- The expression *white as snow* is used in reference to the pure, clean, and innocent.
- The term *whiteout* means zero visibility.

- The phrase *white flag* is associated with meanings of surrender and relinquishment.
- The term *white elephant* refers to a rare or valuable item that is unwanted.
- The expression *pearly whites* refers to very white teeth.
- The term *whitewash* has meanings of cover-up, secrecy, and concealment.
- The term *white list* is a list of acceptable, good, or approved items.
- The term *white sale* means a store sale of sheets, towels, and other linens.
- The term *white knight* represents one who comes to the rescue, a good and noble hero.
- The term *white lightning* refers to moonshine or illegal whiskey.
- The expression *white knuckle* references something that is fast, exciting, or frightening.

Whether consciously or subconsciously, these images of black and white are supplanted into our minds. Self-worth, self-value, and self-esteem play a vital role in the development of many of our children. People are not born to stereotype, hate, judge, or discriminate. These personal attributes are developed and taught. During their developmental stages, children are very impressionable. Whatever is placed inside of their minds and hearts will surely impact the kind of person they will become. Once adulthood is reached, I believe the developed personal personas and traits of individuals take on a whole new way of thinking. I have always advocated the desire to be treated as an individual, not as a black man. Prior to developing a preconceived opinion of anyone, I have relied on each individual person to determine how I would relate to them. To receive respect, you must first give respect. This reciprocal approach has been a guiding principle throughout my life.

For many of us, black versus white offers a mental depiction of all things that are opposite, contrasting, and conflicting. What is the impact of having to endure the effects of these symbolic stereotypes and meanings daily, and how do they affect the hearts and minds of the human spirit? Do these innocent, yet deep symbolic stereotypes and meanings adversely affect how we view and accept each other? What effect do symbolic stereotypes have on real or perceived threats, feelings, and the actions of people? Oftentimes, symbolic meanings are allowed to be transformed into actual policy and legislation. As an illustration, gun laws may be viewed as an equalizer for one group—stand your ground—while access to education may be viewed as an equalizer for another. While fear may be the one element that brings one group together, opportunity may be the one element that defines another.

Another example of symbolic meanings transforming into reality is the slow and methodical deterioration of events such as Black History Month. In many schools and areas, it is now called or promoted as Multicultural Month. In other instances, Black History Month has been eliminated altogether. Why is this the case? I can recall, during the first election of Barack Obama, many declared an end to racism. Why was that?

Prior to major civil rights legislation, I can only imagine how many people of color must have felt as if there was no hope. I believe that today, there may be countless people of color who continue to feel despair. Perhaps some of us are not built to endure the long haul. How long can anyone endure being on the so-called bottom rung of society? Living under a constant cloud of discrimination can be overbearing for some. Unable to find a job to support your family, having to deal with an unfair criminal justice system, can't afford many of life's essentials let alone any luxuries, and having to deal with a constant barrage of racial stereotyping can only dampen your resolve after being beaten down and treated like a substandard citizen on a day-to-day basis. I know this to be true because after working in an industry where there weren't very many people who looked like me, particularly in management, I felt challenged almost daily, as if I had to prove myself to others that I was just as capable as any other man in doing whatever I was charged to do. My challenges never turned to despair, but I did experience weariness. There were times when I can recall sitting in my vehicle in the parking lot prior to entering my office, pumping myself up with what I'd call a "spiritual pep rally." I felt I needed to do this to motivate myself in preparing for whatever challenges I'd encounter on that particular day. Power and prejudice are destructive. Those who practice this can be relentless in their pursuit.

Even though slavery was abolished in 1865, there are enduring and overwhelming factors between having to deal with a history of racism and bias and modern-day despair. In comparison to what's going on in our modern-day society, I can also imagine how those who were enslaved must have felt overwhelming despair.

Documented history reveals that during the approximate three-week journey involving the Middle Passage—transatlantic slave trade—many on board jumped to their deaths rather than deal with the harsh realities they were about to endure.

Enslaved men and women killed themselves for a number of different reasons. Many were unable to cope with the long and traumatic journey, which regularly involved beatings, murder, and rape. Some hoped that death would take them back home to Africa.

Committing suicide was also an act of rebellion. The crews of slave ships were always anxious to prevent enslaved people from killing themselves because each person who managed to take their own life reduced the voyage's profits.

Some enslaved men and women refused to eat, hoping to starve themselves to death. This might have involved holding food in their mouths and then spitting it out when the crew wasn't looking, although this could have led to floggings and force-feedings as punishment.

Leaping overboard to drown was another means of escape. There are moving descriptions of enslaved Africans jumping into the sea together, holding hands or embracing until the end.

Enslaved Africans aboard some ships managed to get hold of knives, swords, and even guns and gunpowder. Those who did not turn these weapons on the crew sometimes used them to commit suicide.

Considering the deplorable conditions and being forcefully separated from family and familiar surroundings, many must have felt degradation, humiliation, and despair. If you are not equipped to handle such traumatic circumstances, it is clearly understood how and why despair is and was so prevalent. Perhaps some people may feel that way today.

The opposite of despair is resolve—firm determination to do something. Despair versus resolve. As we have studied and analyzed the impact of slavery in America, have you ever taken the time to ask yourself: How would I have endured in such horrific conditions? As I reflect, many may ask, why do you even think about things like this? Well, I am intrigued by the whole history of my culture, not just the shining, glimmering aspects of perceived present-day accomplishments. Thinking about things like this question is just as important to me as it is to those who commemorate the plight of Native Americans, the Holocaust, internment of Japanese Americans, European immigration in the colonial era, and the Civil War.

My response to the question of how I would have endured under such horrific conditions of slavery is: I don't think I would have endured. My answer has nothing to do with weakness, but in fact has everything to do with strength.

> *You cannot separate peace from freedom because no one can be at peace unless he has his freedom.*
>
> —Malcolm X

How was I shaped and motivated by chapter two?

I have been raised, educated, and trained to pay attention to symbols and non-verbal communications. I have learned that oftentimes there is meaning to the actions of others without a single word having been spoken. The drawback to this approach is bearing the risk of being overly analytical about things you observe and experience. Still, it is advantageous for you to understand the significance of symbols that are perhaps used daily that could or will affect others with deep passion. Oftentimes, racism is delivered in a symbolic, nonverbal fashion. Please understand that, sometimes, symbolic meanings can be intentional or unintentional. What impact, if any, did the slave trade or plantation life have on perpetuating present-day stereotypical symbols? My focus in chapter two is to place emphasis on the intentional nature of symbolic meanings.

While working on this chapter, I am reminded of just how powerful even modern-day symbols can be. To prepare you for what is to come and as you delve deeper into this book, I want to share a few of what I believe are symbols that are so powerful, they can sometimes evoke unchecked rage in some of us. Some examples include:

- The slave trade
- The Nazi symbol
- Black power symbols
- White power symbols
- The Confederate flag and statues
- Images of modern-day Hip-Hop culture and fashion

- Images of white supremacist
- The reality of seeing black males with white females
- The reality of seeing black females with white males
- The symbolic myths associated with black incarceration
- Law enforcement overreach with people of color
- Images of the struggles endured by poor people of color who live in our inner cities and poor rural areas
- Images of people of color who supposedly drain our public assistance programs
- The reality of seeing people of color in corporate, political, or other significant leadership positions

It has been my experience that those who practice racism typically operate in a covert manner, meaning not openly acknowledged or displayed. To counter covert racism, you must first be able to recognize the calculated action of others as well as the impact of modern-day symbols. This is the principal message in chapter two, Black and White—Let's Go Deeper.

CHAPTER 3

Why Talk About This Controversial Topic?

—ᵐ—

Our lives begin to end the day we become
silent about things that matter.
—Martin Luther King Jr.

—ᵐ—

So why talk about race? Why not? Talking about race and racism is important. You can only create viable solutions to difficult problems when you engage in critical conversation with others who may have differing viewpoints. Silence or fear is counterproductive to finding solutions. How will the divide that exists among us be narrowed if we fail to attempt to bridge the gap?

Perhaps the relevant question is what happens if we as a people and as a society fail to address such powerful issues as racism? If unaddressed, differing viewpoints would remain unheard, and full equality would be a farce. If progress is forced or made without including the concerns of all, this progress would be fleeting. Some would argue that fleeting progress is better than no progress. I would argue that inclusion produces optimum outcomes; exclusion has an adverse effect. Who among us has no desire to be heard? Society as a whole is only as great as its weakest link. It does not matter what side of the aisle you stand on; you can still contribute something to the well-being of others.

I am tackling this subject with the full awareness that many of my readers, of all colors, may feel uncomfortable. This is a risk I am willing to take. If not me, then who? If not now, then when? When you consider history—the Middle Passage, slavery, Jim Crow, Civil Rights Act of 1964, the election of Barack Obama as president, present-day race relations, and political climate—instead of a feeling of progress, there can be a feeling of regression.

After the election of the forty-fourth president of the United States, I actually heard people say that his election was the end of racism. I heard others say we now live in a post racial society. After the election of the forty-fifth president of the United States, I don't see how anyone could ignore the fact that there has been a dramatic shift in race relations in this country. In our present-day society, does fairness, justice, morals, integrity, respect, and leading by example matter anymore? Or have we adopted a mind-set where it's about winning, holding on to power at all costs?

According to the Pew Research Center, roughly seven in ten Black Americans (71 percent) say they have personally experienced discrimination or been treated unfairly because of their race or ethnicity, including 11 percent who say this is something they experience regularly. Far lower shares of whites (30 percent) and Hispanics (52 percent) report experiencing discrimination because of their race or ethnicity.

Overall, four in ten Black Americans say their race or ethnicity has made it harder for them to succeed in life, while about half (51 percent) say it hasn't made much difference, and just 8 percent say it has made it easier for them to succeed. One in five Hispanics say their race or ethnicity has made it harder to succeed in life while just 5 percent of white adults say the same, and 31 percent of whites say their race or ethnicity has made it easier for them to succeed.

When asked about specific kinds of discrimination that people may face, about half of black adults said that in the past year, someone has acted as if they were suspicious of them (47 percent) or as if they thought they weren't smart (45 percent). About two in ten blacks say they were treated unfairly in hiring, pay, or promotion over the past year (21 percent), and a similar share (18 percent) say they have been unfairly stopped by the police over the same period. In each of these cases, blacks are more likely than both whites and Hispanics to say they have experienced these things in the past year.

I can recall, very vividly, a conversation I had in my home with a friend. Coincidently, my friend and I had very different political viewpoints. As we were engaged in point-counterpoint conversation about race relations in America, my friend made a comment that I will never forget. He said one of my problems with the race-relations issue was that I did not trust the government enough. Admittedly, I was shocked at his assertion while having to admit how true his assertion was. My response was—and the problem is when you consider historical facts and the history of race relations in America—why would I wholeheartedly trust the government to fully and fairly represent my best interest? For starters, my mistrust may have something to do with documented, historical incidents such as the Tuskegee Syphilis Experiment, lynching, church bombings and burnings, and the Ku Klux Klan. As for my friend, I realized not only are these types of discussions good for encounters with those who are outside of your culture, but they are beneficial for those who are within your culture as well.

My story is just that—my story! My story is no different from your story. Everyone has a story. The question is, what have you done with your story? Did you use your story to grow and mature as a person? Did you use your story to help others? Did you use your story to try to make an impact, a difference? Exercising bias and negative stereotypes are applicable to all ethnic groups. Various forms of racism are exerted by all ethnic groups. To be clear, African Americans exercise racism against non-African Americans as well as each other. In this book, I chose to explore racism from the perspective of the recipient.

I swore never to be silent whenever and wherever human beings endure suffering and humiliation. We must take sides. Neutrality helps the oppressor, never the victim. Silence encourages the tormentor, never the tormented.
—Elie Wiesel

For clarity, let's be clear about the subject matter. What is racism? According to present-day definition, racism is: (1) prejudice, discrimination, or antagonism directed against someone of a different race based on the belief that one's own race is superior; (2) racism is the belief that all members of each race possess characteristics or abilities specific to that race, especially so as to distinguish it as inferior or superior to another race or races. Are there different types of racism? Unequivocally, yes.

Individual or internalized racism. This is racism that exists within individuals. It is when one holds negative ideas about their own culture, even if unknowingly. Xenophobic feelings or one's internalized sense of oppression/privilege are two examples of individual or internalized racism.

Interpersonal racism. This is the racism that occurs between individuals. It is the holding of negative attitudes toward a different race or culture. Interpersonal racism often follows a victim/perpetrator model.

Institutional racism. Recognizing that racism need not be individualist or intentional, institutional racism refers to institutional and cultural practices that perpetuate racial inequality. Benefits are structured to advantage powerful groups at the expense of others. Jim Crow laws and redlining practices are two examples of institutional racism.

Structural racism. Structural racism refers to the ways in which the joint operation of institutions (i.e., interinstitutional arrangements and interactions) produces racialized outcomes, even in the absence of racist intent. Indicators of structural racism include power inequalities, unequal access to opportunities, and differing policy outcomes by race. Because these effects are reinforced across multiple institutions, the root causes of structural racism are difficult to isolate. Structural racism is cumulative, pervasive, and durable.

Diversity in America is here to stay; it's not going away anytime soon. It doesn't really matter if you are for or against diversity; you've got to find a way to deal with it. In education and in the workplace, it is difficult if not next to impossible to bury your head in the sand and act as if the issues of race and racism do not exist. At some point, you've got to come out of your bunker or your hood and deal with people who may not look, act, and think like you.

Even if you attempt to conceal what you feel deep down inside, it is just simply a matter of time before there will be a slow and methodical drain (drip, drip) that will eventually force you out of your warm and fuzzy closet.

Causes of racism include:

- Fear
- Bigotry
- Ignorance
- Hatred
- Upbringing
- Pride
- Envy
- Lack of education
- Desire to belong
- Feeling of entitlement
- A desire to be affiliated with money and power
- A desire to be affiliated with like-minded people
- Insecurity
- Low self-esteem
- Anger
- Lack of empathy
- A desire to suppress and dominate
- Greed

In my view, as an African American, we are expected to survive and function in two different environments—two different worlds. We've got to work in environments where, oftentimes on the surface, diversity, inclusiveness, and political correctness is expected. Our reality is often encountering an environment where workplace politics, racism, and discrimination thrives. In our minds and hearts, many of us are fully aware what we are up against. We must constantly put up a shield, a defense. It's a facade. It's called tolerance and awareness. It's seething under your breath at every intentional and unintentional racist act, comment, and action. There appears to be some sort of obsession from others in the workplace on why our looks, thoughts, mannerisms, and views are so different.

If you work in an environment where you are the minority, you've got to make others feel as if you are non-threatening! As I have analyzed the dynamics of forming teams and participated in hiring practices within the workplace, I can't emphasize enough how critical it is for minorities to put their supervisors and coworkers at ease in the workplace. There's no sugarcoating this revelation. This reality is rarely spoken, but for those of us who are battle-tested, we know this to be true. You see, hiring and firing decisions are often made based on a certain comfort level with a potential candidate or employee.

At the end of the day, we return to our homes where the daily events of our spouses, children, and friends are similar to ours, be it on a slightly different scale. Those who we interact with at work or leisure, who look like us, generally do not perceive us as a threat. Generally, we don't place great emphasis on power, position, authority, job title, and how much money you make. What we really care about is fairness. Are you consistent with all when interacting and engaging people? Are you real? Can you relate? Success is fine; just don't forget where you come from. Are you humble? Do you have empathy for the less fortunate? Do you care?

W. E. B. Du Bois Called It What?

Understanding W. E. B. Du Bois's Concept of Double Consciousness

> *It is a peculiar sensation, the double-consciousness, this sense of always looking for one's self through the eyes of others…one ever feels his twoness, an American, a Negro; two souls, two thoughts, two unreconciled strivings; two warring ideals in one dark body whose dogged strength alone keeps it from being torn asunder.*
>
> —W. E. B. Du Bois

In the view of Dr. W. E. B. Du Bois, sociologist, civil rights activist, historian, and author, double consciousness is a concept that Du Bois first explores in the 1903 publication *The Souls of Black Folk*. Double consciousness describes the individual sensation of feeling as though your identity is divided into several parts, making it difficult or impossible to have one unified identity. Du Bois spoke of this within the context of race relations in the United States. He asserted that since American blacks have lived in a society that has historically repressed and devalued them, it has become difficult for them to unify their black identity with their American identity. Double consciousness forces blacks to not only view themselves from their own unique perspective but also to view themselves as they might be perceived by the outside world. This is what Du Bois spoke of in the above passage when he talked about "the sense of looking at one's self through the eyes of others."

As a result, blacks can suffer from a damaged self-image shaped by the perceptions and treatment of white people. Black life in turn can easily become shaped by stereotypes perpetuated by mainstream culture.

Double consciousness also creates an element of conflict within the Black American, as we struggle—often unsuccessfully—to reconcile our identity as a black person and as an American citizen.

Double consciousness is still very relevant to contemporary society. While many people would like to argue that we live in a post racial society, there are still many inequalities based on race that make it difficult for Black Americans to reconcile our identities as blacks and as Americans. Our media sells us images of black men as athletes, rappers, or criminals, and as a result white America perceives black men as such, and young black males see these limited paths as their only options for advancement. This is just one illustration of how the media, which is largely dominated by white executives, continues to assume the role of shaping the perceptions that blacks have of themselves—and that whites have of blacks.

My millennial or Gen Y daughters and mentees have taught me a new term: code switching. It means to customize style of speech to the audience or group being addressed. Corporately and individually, you adjust your speech to the audience. You may alter your speech to accommodate whatever particular group you are dealing with. I do not view this behavior as hypocritical; I view this behavior as a necessary survival technique. The term may be new; however, the concept is the same.

Whether you are supportive or non-supportive of a diverse environment, your children and future generations must possess the skill set to engage diversity. The facts of expanding diversity and technology are the catalyst for this reality. Having the ability to navigate in, around, and through diverse personal, professional, and social environments is an essential life skill.

I believe America is justifiably judged rather harshly for its actions/inactions of dealing with racism during the first three decades of this century. How did we arrive at the point we are at today? Considering the majority's viewpoint, is there a desire to protect white privilege and entitlement? Or is there a desire to hold on to power and money? Hate? Post-Obama backlash? Is there a pursuit to maintain a majority status? From a minority perspective, is it acceptance of mediocrity and complacency? Lethargic? Apathy? Fear? Low self-esteem and low self-worth? Lack of education? Despair? Lack of opportunity? Disillusion? Ignorance? I frequently remind others that the view looking down is vastly different from the view looking up.

On an almost daily basis, we are presented with some mind-boggling, head-scratching news impacting injustice, race and racism. For many of us who grew up in the '50s, '60s, and '70s, it's as if the hands of time have been turned back. What changed? What happened?

I am not a cultural anthropologist. However, I do find the present-day racial and cultural phenomenon intriguing. I am suggesting that going back to the days of Jim Crow, up to the present day, not much has changed. What we are experiencing today is a divide that has been lying dormant. It is an evolution. Gasoline has been poured on a smoldering, simmering flicker that has suddenly erupted again. Change on the surface was a facade. If you are honest, you will acknowledge that over the last fifteen to twenty years, there has been a slow and methodical effort to dismantle many of the social gains that were achieved during the '70s, '80s, and '90s. I could site many references, but is there really a need to? Okay, I couldn't resist: the current political climate, police profiling, law enforcement brutalizing and killing people of color, the justice system, prison populations, diminishing civil rights, and stricter voter registration laws.

You may feel as if I am demonizing whites while allowing blacks to be portrayed as victims. Two noteworthy comments:

1. I cannot and do not speak for any specific ethnic group. My thoughts are reflective of my view of society, not a specific group. There are good and bad people in every group.
2. We all tend to view life from the viewpoint of our personal prism, our perspective. Our personal prism is affected by our experiences, environment, upbringing, education, beliefs, and ethics.

As I reflect on all the injustices that I have seen and experienced over the years, should I or did I have the right to lash out? This is a fundamental question that males of color must ask themselves, even today. The answer is an unequivocal *no*. From a spiritual perspective, the written word speaks clearly of how to handle vengeance and forgiveness. From a secular or worldly perspective, when you lash out, you give others power over you. For every action, there is a reaction. When you lash out, there are great risks and consequences associated with doing so. As previously stated, there are thoughtful and calculated ways to handle perceived injustices. I would suggest you learn the system, processes, and the law and understand individual rights so that you can place yourself in the best possible position to safely and legally overcome challenges that will most certainly come your way. In these types of situations, your decision-making and self-discipline are key.

I felt obligated to talk about what to do if you experience racism. I had no intentions of taking on a *what to do if* advisory role. I would have felt somewhat conflicted if I had not mentioned this; perhaps there would have been a feeling of incompleteness. Again, my purpose was to share, encourage, and enlighten, not to advise.

So what do you do if you experience racism? How do you address racism? What agencies are available to help? Keep in mind that just because someone has a belief of or in racism, this does not mean that you have been discriminated against. A belief does not constitute that a law has been broken. If or when a person's belief turns into discriminatory actions or conduct, then there is a possible recourse to formally address your concerns. There is no *one size fits all* answer. Make no mistake, this issue is or can become a very complex issue. The who, what, when, where, how, and level of frequency must initially be addressed. Is the issue work related, business related, or of a personal nature? Options can be as broad and complex as the issue. You can opt to do nothing, talk to a trusted confidant, or file a complaint with the Equal Employment Opportunity Commission (EEOC). On a personal note, I am an advocate of trying to solve any problem at the lowest level possible first.

As I have previously stated, for me, any potential claim or consideration of discrimination was considered only after all other logic, rationales, and justifications had failed. For me, this was a last-resort approach. Always examine your own actions as well; ensure your motives and feelings are not biased.

In addition to state-level workforce commissions and the EEOC, other options include but are not limited to:

- Personal legal representation
- Individual corporate, business, or government ethics offices
- Human resources department of applicable company, organizations, government agencies, or schools

Even though there is a federal law against retaliation after a formal complaint has been filed, realistically expect some sort of retribution in this situation. Others will become defensive—very defensive. Documentation, witnesses, and electronic evidence will most certainly help your situation.

How was I shaped and motivated by chapter three?

The mind is like a parachute—it works best when open. If change is ever going to occur to better race relations and end racism, how is this change possible without dialogue? The level of potential controversy in any given topic should not act as a deterrent in our attempt to seek improvements or solutions. Dialogue begins and ends with respect. We do not have to always agree with one another, but we should be able to listen to the issues without fear of retaliation, intimidation, and threats. Let me also mention that fair and impartial dialogue involves recognizing truth. Further, recognizing truth means the outcome may not necessarily support your point of view. Race and racism are front and center of our everyday lives. We can attempt to marginalize this issue, but it will not work. As a result of non-engagement, nothing improves without real dialogue. Here in chapter three, this is the message being conveyed.

CHAPTER 4

Various Encounters with Race and Racism

———∞∞———

We must learn to live together as brothers or perish together as fools.
—Martin Luther King Jr.

———∞∞———

FOR MANY OF US, RACE and racism are uniquely linked to history. Depending on your age, many of us can still remember images of the bombings in Birmingham, the march from Selma, Rosa Parks refusing to sit in the back of the bus, and the many challenges faced by Reverend Dr. Martin Luther King Jr. Some of us may feel our association with these images is limited to documentaries and the history books. If true, this thought process is as far from the truth as can be. While we are fully aware of the documented accounts of our history involving race and racism, if we would only ask, we would discover that so many of us have untold stories that are just as impactful as some of the well-documented historical accounts. Our individual and personal struggles involving race and racism may not warrant national attention, but nonetheless they are just as impactful and meaningful to us, no matter the level of exposure.

Through living my life, perhaps just like you, I have discovered that racism is as alive today as it was during the lifetime of our dear ancestors who were born during the first thirty years of the nineteenth century. The dynamics of how racism is viewed and executed have changed, but the impact and overall end results remain the same for present-day society. In the past, many racist experiences were obvious, overt, right in your face, front and centered. In many cases today, the execution of racism has taken on more of a covert, concealed form. I would even suggest that many of us today experience difficulty in detecting covert racism. I can't fully explain why this is the case, but I can say without hesitation that I have worked with others who were oblivious to the covert racism around them. Ironically today, as a nation and as a people, in many ways we have returned to our covert past.

To illustrate the impact of race and racism, I have lifted several incidents from my own life. While identifying the negative, I have also chosen to accentuate how I grew as an individual as a result of my experiences.

Number one: My mother couldn't give birth in the hospital.

During the era in which I was born, it was still taboo for African American mothers to give birth in hospitals. After all, this was the rural Florida Panhandle in the late '50s. The norm or options for African American mothers were to give birth at home in the presence of midwives, grandmothers, aunts, and elderly friends. Consequently, it was against established protocol for black children to be born in the local hospital. While discussing this project with a family member, I was reminded that there was an all-black hospital ward across the state line, in Georgia, for expectant African American mothers. This may have been the only hospital option within a seventy-five-mile radius.

What did I learn from this experience?

Aside from shared stories from my mother prior to her death, there are no learning experiences that I can personally relate to. However, as I absorb history and passed down facts, I cannot help but wonder in amazement of the acceptable norms of our society during this part of American history. I can only imagine how nonexistent prenatal care was for expectant African American mothers. I can only imagine how many babies of color were lost due to high-risk pregnancies and unexpected emergencies while giving birth at home. The anxiety and comparisons of what was permitted for one race of people versus what was not permitted for another must have been so disheartening. Amazingly, our foreparents endured. This is the takeaway: how adversity, racism, injustice, suffering, and inequality were so prevalent, yet those impacted by it endured! This is truly astonishing.

No matter the situation, I've learned to persevere. Enduring does not have to be indefinite; however, I had to persevere until there was a glimmer of light that enabled me to break through whatever stronghold I happened to be dealing with.

Number two: I watched my mother go to work as a domestic worker.

My mother was a maid, a domestic worker for those who could afford to hire one. I can recall my mother working for three different families at various intervals. The one memory that has been permanently etched in my brain is watching my mother being picked up by her employer. At the time I must have been about ten years old, but I can recall standing in the front of the house during the summer months, watching as my mother was picked up by her employer. The older white female employer was alone, as my mother was required to sit in the back seat alone. Two people in the car, one white female who was driving and one black female who was not allowed to sit in the vacant front seat. As I reflect on witnessing this, I can recall having a weird feeling in the pit of my stomach. For my young readers, I assure you this was not an Uber-type pickup. At the time, I did not fully understand it, but I knew something did not sit well with what I was witnessing. For further insight, please refer to appendix three.

What did I learn from this experience?

My mother's priority was providing for and supporting her children. She worked with what she had to work with. She was dedicated. She was determined. She was driven by a higher purpose. Her employers were kind to her. They were kind to her because I believe she had high morals, ethics, and work standards. As a result, her employers went above and beyond for her. I can recall my mother being given hand-me-down clothes, excess food, and other things that she could use to help support her four children. My mother was the most impactful person in my life.

I do recall receiving government assistance for food; however, we never stayed in government subsidized housing. My mother understood the significance of caring for her needy children. She made sacrifices. She humbled herself. In the end, it was not about her; it was about her four children.

It is because of her sacrifices I was compelled to go above and beyond for her once I became an adult and was financially able to do so. My primary takeaway from this experience was an understanding that it is often necessary to sacrifice for those you love, meaning to place the concerns of others above your own concerns and well-being.

Number three: the local movie theater
As a child during the late '60s, my hometown had one movie theater. Whites were allowed to sit on the main ground floor of the theater while blacks were relegated to the balcony. This was my first exposure to segregation. Obviously, the seating in the balcony was cramped, and the site lines were not optimum. I do recall some contentious incidents, but they never resulted or escalated into fights. While attending the theater, African Americans were most engaged when black movies were shown. This is when I first saw the movies *Shaft*, *In the Heat of the Night*, *Buck and the Preacher*, *Super Fly*, and *Coffey*, all classic African American movies. The amazing thing about this situation is that I cannot recall when the segregation in the movie theater ended.

What did I learn from this experience?
At the time, my feelings were that's just the way it was. As a child, I did not fully comprehend the impact of this situation. I just knew this is the way it was in my hometown. This was the system. The impact of this situation did not really hit me until I left home and had exposure to other areas of the country. I discovered these other towns and cities were totally opposite of what I had experienced in my hometown. This is when I knew that the racial practices in my hometown were not a reflection of what other more progressive towns, cities, and states were experiencing. This is when I knew I could never live in such an environment again.

Number four: Summer camp
This event occurred in the 1960s. My oldest sister's brother-in-law and next-door neighbor, Coach Johnson, was an educator at one of the all-black schools in one of the smaller neighboring towns. My youngest sister and I spent part of our summer vacations attending summer school/camp that was supervised by this very dedicated and patient man. In these camps we would have activities, play sports,

games, and take field trips. The one standout event of summer school/camp was our occasional trips to the public pool. There was just one little problem with our visits to the public pool: my hometown had only one public pool, and it was not an integrated pool. Blacks were not allowed in my hometown's only public pool. Coach Johnson and staff had worked out an arrangement where we would travel approximately thirty-five miles by school bus to a neighboring town and state to enjoy swimming in a public pool. This particular public pool was located at an all-black community center. As I reflect, the irony of having black kids in one state having to travel to another more conservative town and state to swim in a public pool was somewhat mind-boggling.

What did I learn from this experience?
During that era, amazingly, Alabama—the neighboring state—of all places was more progressive in certain quality of life areas than my home state of Florida. Even though this recreational activity was unavailable in my hometown, the actions of Coach Johnson and the administrators who employed him had the determination and foresight to seek alternatives. The actions of those who practiced segregated polices did not deter these adults who were determined to make sure black children had equal access to similar recreational activities regardless of the actions and efforts they had to endure. The primary lesson learned from this experience is that there are alternative and thoughtful ways to overcome bigotry through civil and thoughtful ways. It is not always necessary to meet force with force. Seek amicable solutions through the appropriate channels. Also, as I grew older, I developed an appreciation for what Coach Johnson had to endure: a busload of rambunctious children. He handled us with calmness and a smile.

Number five: Transitioning from an all-black to an integrated school
During the mid to late 1960s, I went to an all-black public school from elementary to seventh grade. The one all-black public school housed students from first grade through twelfth grade. In comparison, the white children had two elementary schools, grades one through six, and one high school that accommodated white children in grades seven through twelve. Please note that during this era, going to an all-black school and an all-white school was not a school of choice issue. This was a segregated system. By my seventh grade year, the law changed to

school choice. As I recall, a small percentage of African Americans opted to attend or integrate with the all-white schools during that first year. The following year, my eighth grade year, full school integration was the law.

Once I became an adult, I moved away from my hometown. Years later, on one of many return visits, I had an opportunity to visit with one of my favorite former teachers who happened to be a long-tenured and well-respected educator. It was during one of these visits that she openly discussed the stark and contrasting differences between the educational realities involving white versus black students.

Obviously, she pointed out how the discrepancies or the disparities in pay between black and white educators impacted the morale of those who were on the negative side of this reality. The difference in the maintenance of the facilities was visible for all to see. The classroom furniture and equipment were substandard for the all-black schools. The sports uniforms were subpar. My former teacher even went to great lengths to explain the difference in the grades of toilet tissue given to the all-black schools versus the all-white schools. As a child, I can recall never having new textbooks in school. Our textbooks required each student to sign their names on the back, inside cover of each book. By the time these textbooks were given to us and before we signed our names, there were easily four to five prior signatures of students from the white schools. This meant that by the time these textbooks were distributed to the African American students and schools, the textbooks were four to five years old. I knew this to be true because when I arrived on the white campus for the first time, I personally witnessed the stark differences and was in awe.

What did I learn from this experience?
At the time, African Americans accepted this as their reality. Segregation was the law. Once this law changed, it was met with mixed emotions from the black community. As a young child and prior to the change in the law, I can recall some forms of protest. I can recall participating in a civil rights march in the state capital. As I reflect, there wasn't any bloodshed or beatings, but there was a deep feeling of injustice. There was a purposeful, spiritual connection to this experience. I don't know for sure, but I am confident that the white community had mixed emotions as well. Worth noting, it was about this time when private, white

schools began to flourish. The students handled this transition better than the adults did. I can recall two to three years after initial integration, it was somewhat accepted to befriend someone of a different race. This was my first real interaction with white kids.

Number six: A coach—the first confrontation and falsehood with an authority figure

I can remember vividly having to confront a coach about perceived injustices. This coach was the first adult in a position of authority who I felt misrepresented his words. One example is that there were people selected for the team who shouldn't have been selected; let's just say they were connected. As a player, if you did not embrace this decision 100 percent, you were singled out. After an encounter on the bench during one particular game, the coach formed an opinion about my perceived less-than-enthusiastic cheering and support. The next week, the team was sitting on the bus, getting ready to depart for an away game. The coach walks on the bus and, in front of the other players, tells me to get off the bus. The coach claims he had told me previously that I would not be allowed to make the trip. Keep in mind, I had practiced and was in the gym at least an hour prior to departure. This was like a sucker punch to the gut for a young teenager. I did not know how to deal with this issue; I simply walked away, never to play again. My athletic dreams were crushed. As time passed, I let out my frustrations by beating up on others in pick-up games. Years later, a former teammate approached me to let me know that he wished he had had the courage that I had displayed by refusing to beg my way back on the team after being unjustly singled out by the coach.

I can also recall a situation where I was told not to hang out—outside of sports—with certain people. None of my hanging out friends had a police record. None of my hanging out friends were problem-makers at school. None of my hanging out friends were gang members. The worst activities my hanging out friends were engaged in were liking girls and smoking cigarettes. I felt conflicted about playing sports and being told who to befriend and who not to befriend. Giving the coach the benefit of the doubt, maybe he was looking out for my best interest; I will never know. What I do know is it didn't feel right, and if I would have had an adult to talk to me about this situation, the outcome may have been a little different.

What did I learn from this experience?

If there was anything positive that could have been gleamed out of this situation at the time, it would have been that an adult (parent) was needed for this situation. I chose not to tell my mother because in my heart I knew she was too busy doing life, trying to deal with everyday issues. This memory was forever etched in my brain. It did not occur to me until I started writing this book that when the coach told me I shouldn't hang out with certain people, it was because some of my friends during this time were white. Could it be that I was misguided all these years, puzzled about why this would be said about my black friends when the problem could have easily been my white friends? When I became a parent, I made a conscience decision to fully engage with all school-related activities. Because my daughters were placed in a school environment where they were truly the minority, I am completely convinced that my children benefitted immensely from the hands on approach taken by my wife and me.

Number seven: First African American homecoming queen

As previously mentioned, I attended a segregated school through the seventh grade. During my senior year of high school, the high school crowned its first African American homecoming queen. The homecoming queen's victory was somewhat of a shock to the African American students. The homecoming queen elected two young men to escort her. Again, to the best of my memory, this was the first time in history that a homecoming queen elected two escorts. The homecoming queen selected me as one of her two escorts.

As I reflect on the homecoming queen's decision, this may have revealed that she had tremendous foresight. Typically, at high school football games, the black students and black parents sat on opposite ends of the home team side of the stands from those of the white student body and white families. The marching band and cheerleaders were always positioned in front of the white student body and white families. The homecoming queen made the decision that we would sit near the marching band, cheerleaders, white student body, and white families. During the course of the homecoming game, we were heckled, and on at least one occasion a raw egg was thrown at us. The raw egg did not hit its intended targets. We did not retaliate. In afterthought, my co-escort and I were there to protect the homecoming queen. We blanketed her from the time she arrived until she departed.

What did I learn from this experience?
This was my very first exposure to acceptance of the fact that African American young ladies could be recognized for their beauty, brains, and personality. To this day, I am not sure why the homecoming queen picked me as one of her escorts, but it began to make me look at myself from a different perspective. I never had the opportunity to talk to the homecoming queen about the historic impact of her selection, but I was humbled that she invited me to take part in something that was incredible for her. As you might imagine, my friends gave me a very hard time about escorting the homecoming queen.

Number eight: Working at a local family discount store
During the early '70s, the best jobs available for young African American teenagers in my hometown were agriculture labor, fast-food restaurants, janitorial, bagging groceries, or pumping gas at a local gas station. I cannot recall exactly how employment was gained, but somehow as a teenager I was able to secure a job working at a local discount department store. My duties and responsibilities included stocking shelves, unloading trucks, putting displays together, and general cleaning. At some point during my employment, I gained the trust of the general manager. She decided to train me to operate the cash register. This meant trusting me with money and interacting with all customers. In a small rural town in the '70s, a job of this nature for a young African American was unheard of. The remainder of the staff included middle-aged white females. The general manager and staff were fair and generous to me. One startling revelation was the general manger often called the school and was able to get me released from classes to report to work to unload trucks.

What did I learn from this experience?
Make no mistake about this employment opportunity, I was very fortunate to have this opportunity. Even though I was quite young at the time, this opportunity positively impacted my outlook about opportunity and race. In fact, upon my pending graduation from high school, the general manager encouraged me to consider advancement in the company by pursuing in-house educational advancement opportunities for a general manager position. I was grateful, but the vision I had for myself was greater. The general manager saw potential;

she did not see race. This experience gave me a glimmer of hope about future opportunities.

Number nine: The decision to work for the government

I knew it. I felt it. I saw it. During the '70s and earlier, if you were African American, working for the government afforded you certain job securities and quality of life advantages that may not have been otherwise available. I knew men who were military veterans, or worked for the state of Florida. I knew women who were educators employed by the school system. There was something distinctly different about these men and women that I could not quite put my finger on. Working in a government-related job appeared to offer African Americans a higher standard of living. They carried themselves in a somewhat dignified way. They appeared to be well-rounded. They were respected by others within the community. There were visible intangibles that I could not explain. I came to understand that working for the government afforded African Americans better employment opportunities. The job security, fairness, and benefits were unparalleled. This became my aiming point because growing up in a small town, rural community did not provide exposure into corporate America.

What did I learn from this experience?

Whatever these career government men and women had, I wanted too; I wanted to emulate what I saw and felt. Once I finished high school, I looked for options. I knew there was more to life than what my hometown offered. As a result, I decided to enlist in the US Army. Twenty years later, I was and am now confident that the decision to enlist was one of the wisest decisions I could have made at that time. The experience gained from my military career led to a second successful career.

As I lived and worked in other parts of the country, I discovered that there were some definite truths to my beliefs. I encountered older African Americans who had opted to work for the railroad and postal service. These older African Americans fit the profile of others that I had witnessed earlier in life. During this period of American history, working for any form of government afforded greater opportunities, job security, fairness, benefits, and pensions that at the time were unmatched by the private sector. To a degree, some of those same realities hold true today. The government continues to be a leading employer and offers tremendous opportunities for a large percentage of minorities.

Number ten: Commercial passenger, incident one

During the early '80s, I recall flying out of one of the small regional airports near my hometown; I won't say which one. I had confirmed seat assignments throughout each connection of my flight. My preference is to always sit in an aisle seat, adjacent to the wings, no matter the model of the plane. Well, after receiving my boarding pass and actual boarding got underway, I quickly realized that my seat assignment had been changed to the very last, non-reclining seat on the small prop plane, next to the restroom. I was livid, but I did not want to create a scene on the plane out of fear of being denied the opportunity to fly on to my next destination. When I arrived at my next destination, the customer service supervisor could not explain why this happened and offered an apology. It took every fiber in my body to refrain from getting arrested. Okay, so as the reader, you are wondering, was I the only person of color on the flight? The answer is yes!

What did I learn from this experience?

Proper restraint. Understanding when and how to apply proper restraint is critical to the overall well-being of a person of color. Was it worth causing all hell to break loose? Usually, once I've identified and made others aware of their nonthreatening wrongdoing or oversight, I can sometimes just walk away. Honestly, I did consider notifying the airline's corporate headquarters.

Number eleven: My experiences as a sports official while living in the Pacific Northwest

During the '80s and '90s, I lived in the Pacific Northwest. The demographics, culture, and social and economic makeup of the Pacific Northwest was drastically different from the Deep South. According to the Office of Financial Management, the 2016 population of Washington State was 5,774,206 white and 285,904 black. You can surmise that during my time there in the '80s, the demographics were substantially different—less minorities—than what the 2016 report revealed. During my time there, most of the African American population was concentrated in the state's two largest urban areas, Seattle and Tacoma.

I spent a substantial amount of time refereeing basketball and softball in small rural areas of the state. It was very common for me to officiate a basketball game where the gymnasium was packed with fans and players who were predominately white. I might add that my officiating partners were mostly white as well. My softball umpiring experience was essentially the same. While the fan base of high school basketball was mostly students, the fan base for softball was mostly adults. The irony of this experience is while officiating, I cannot recall one single race-related incident. In fact, as an outsider I was able to advance up the officiating chain to attain rankings in the upper tier of the local sports organizations. I also recall various schools requesting my participation in their sporting events during Black History Month and/or during the periods around Martin Luther King Jr. Day. In certain areas of the state, there was a large Native American population. I loved the time I spent in these areas with Native Americans.

I can recall having numerous conversations with my fellow basketball and softball officiating partners. Most of my partners were intrigued by the opportunity to engage in diverse interactions and conversations. As you might imagine, this change of attitude and contrast from the rural Deep South to the Pacific Northwest was welcomed by me.

What did I learn from this experience?
The people from the Pacific Northwest were fantastic. The attitudes of those who reside in the Pacific Northwest were more liberal than populations in other parts of the country. During my time there, my approach was if you wanted to get respect, you must give and show respect. To become a quality sports official, I worked hard to be the best I could be. I truly believe that I was rewarded for my hard work. The school administrators and coaches recognized efficiency and production and simply saw me as an instrument for fairness. Also, I was selected to be the first African American to umpire behind the plate at the state softball championship level. The actions of the people of the state of Washington touched me deeply.

Number twelve: You live where?
I purchased my home twenty-four years ago in a neighborhood that was about 80 percent Anglo American. I very vividly recall a conversation with one of my

neighbors that shook me at my core. My neighbor indicated that he did not think racism existed. After analyzing his comments, I came to an understanding of exactly why his viewpoint was true. Don't panic; hear me out. This particular neighbor went to a distinguished college that was predominantly white. He lived in a neighborhood that was predominantly white. His kids went to a predominantly white, private school. His place of worship was predominantly white. He worked for a Fortune 500 company that was predominantly white. Most of his colleagues, friends, and those he routinely interacted with were predominantly white. As a result of these truths, he had a very limited exposure to racism. His opinions were primarily shaped by his environment and perspective.

What did I learn from this experience?

Even though my neighbor may have been somewhat naive about what was going on outside of his utopia, I was forced to acknowledge and evaluate his comments from his perspective. Even though I did not agree with him after much dialogue, it forced me to be open minded about his viewpoint. He listened and accepted my counterpoints. I learned that a mind is like a parachute—it works best when open. To this day, I welcome open conversations with others. I've learned that rational conversation with others can be a pathway to understanding.

Number thirteen: Commercial passenger, incident two

As we all know, Southwest Airlines has an open seating policy. The plane's seating configuration was three seats on either side of the center aisle (Boeing 727). As I settled into my seat and prior to takeoff for the coastal Florida panhandle, I realized that I was the only passenger who did not have a seating partner. As I looked around, most of the seats had two to three passengers in each row. Hygiene is never an issue with me, no overbearing cologne, and casual, conservative attire was worn. As I looked around, I just happened to be the only person of color on the plane. Was this sheer coincidence? I simply smiled, sat back, and enjoyed the flight minus having to worry about fighting for the armrest on an hour-and-a-half flight.

What did I learn from this experience?

As previously stated, I only use race in any given situation as an absolute last resort. I struggle with sharing a learning experience from this incident. If anything, this was 2010, and to acknowledge what I was thinking was like a re-boot for my reality hard drive. In fact, if you were to Google information about the coastal Florida panhandle, you will discover that this area and particularly the beaches along the Emerald coast from Pensacola to Panama City are also referred to as the "Redneck Riviera," alluding to the strong Southern culture of the hinterland.

Number fourteen: Slave plantation tour

Somewhere around 2013, my wife and I took one of our many trips to New Orleans. I'm not sure why, but we decided we would take a plantation tour. Coincidently, we were the only African Americans on the tour. No, we were not uncomfortable. After touring four plantations along the Mississippi Delta, we discovered the different plantation tour guides had one of two perspectives. One perspective was to narrate the tour from the plantation owner's perspective, and the second was to narrate the tour from the slave experience. Ironically, a large percentage of the tour participants were from Canada and Europe.

What did I learn from this experience?

After sharing my experience with family and friends, I discovered that for many, such a tour is too painful. For us, the experience was more spiritual. We went in with eyes wide open. One astonishing takeaway was we learned that up until the late 1970s, descendants of slaves still lived on the plantations until new property owners forced them to leave. We were told the slave descendants felt as if they had no place else to go, or they were simply afraid to leave. First of all, I thought to myself, how sad; and secondly, I thought to myself how this revelation is indica-tive of the (symbolic) mental state of many African Americans today. We are free, yet we live as if we are still enslaved.

How was I shaped and motivated by chapter four?

After writing chapter four, I don't think a lot of commentary is needed. It's like a follow-up speaker in church attempting to summarize an awesome sermon by the pastor. Just leave it alone; the sermon spoke for itself.

As I reflect on chapter four, the one prominent reality that cannot be over-looked is that, for me as well as many other people of color, the struggle begins at birth. Unfortunately, and in all likelihood, this struggle may continue throughout the lives of black and brown people in America.

All experiences, good and bad, have something you can gain from them. This is what is being communicated in this chapter. Flip the negative into a positive; use the negativity as motivation. Strive to prove the doubters and the naysayers wrong. Don't become a lifelong victim to a temporary emotional reaction. Look for the positive or lessons learned in each situation; it will definitely make you a better person. Remember, others may be waiting for you to give up or screw up.

CHAPTER 5

Race and Racism in the Workplace

—ɯ—

Racism is man's gravest threat to man—the
maximum of hatred for a minimum of reason.
—Abraham Heschel

—ɯ—

POLITICS, RELIGION, SEX, AND RACE are the controversial issues of our time. Generally, people refrain from talking about these issues in the workplace and among others. In the eyes of many, the feeling of being hesitant to speak on these issues is justified. Generally, talking about any of these topics is viewed as controversial and invokes feelings of deep passion, unimaginable sensitivity, and close-to-the-heart personal beliefs. I believe it is appropriate to avoid talking about these issues in the workplace unless you have been directly impacted because a law or policy has been violated. Avoidance, however, does not mean nonexistence.

For people of color, encountering prejudice and racism in the workplace is not some made-up fantasy; it is alive and well. For many minorities who are professionals and work in a corporate environment, dealing with racism is often dealt with as an unspoken and internal reality. The negative impact exists; the consequences are rarely and openly discussed or displayed. In my conversations with business professions, I have concluded that the so-called race card is only played as a last resort. Executives, senior-level managers, mangers, and entrepreneurs knew

41

that when or if they played this card, it usually resulted in the beginning of the end of the game. Some may claim that the race card is always played, but my experiences are this is not true. I will acknowledge, however, that playing the race card may have been more prevalent among rank and file employees. If I were to speculate, the reason for this is they may have felt as if no one had their backs. So in their minds, there was no other recourse.

The reason for sensitivity or a lack of sensitivity is not complex. As a member of the minority, during our daily lives, we are forced to dine at the table while at work, interact, support, and engage those who are in charge. However, in the daily lives of members of the majority, they are not forced, or there may not be a need for them to sit down at the table and dine with us. By further explanation, when you control politics, education, business, employment, finance, and even entertainment, the rules are tilted toward success for those who control each mentioned segment. I personally struggle with any human being expressing hatred for another human being simply because of the color of one's skin. This type of hatred is deep rooted.

It would lead one to ask the question: Where does this type of feeling come from? Is it an issue of the heart? Upbringing? Learned behavior? This revelation is both scary and sad if you really examine it. Amazingly, I have lived and worked all over the world, and this hatred for people of color persists wherever I have lived and traveled. It is not limited to a region, country, or continent; it is worldwide. I have discovered that in the world of business, various companies, organizations, and even churches publicly embraces diversity and cultural awareness and probably has a lawyer-friendly discrimination policy, but the everyday practices are distinctly different from the actual legal policies. Are corporate core values, diversity, and ethics policy statements worth the paper they are written on? My personal experiences and feelings are mixed. Mostly, I believe these statements are oftentimes used as legal cover and protection rather than to govern the day-to-day actions of a particular company, organization, and their personnel. It appears that whenever a company faces a public relations crisis in this area, because one of their employees went off the rail, they almost always trip over themselves to share with or remind the public what their official policy states. The problem is these companies or organizations do not hold their executives and managers accountable on a day-to-day basis until it's too late. Just paying lip service to any particular problem has never set well with me.

What happened to American society between the Civil Rights Act of 1964 and the end of President Barack Obama's presidency? We knew where we stood as a country prior to the Civil Rights Act. This was a period in history that was defined by overt racism. Though problems remained, many felt as if tremendous growth was attained from the late '60s through 2016. After 2016, many would perceive a significant paradigm shift. I am suggesting that very little changed from pre-1964 through 2016.

The Workplace—Overview

In my chosen career field, there were not very many people of color in management or supervisory positions. I primarily attribute this to a lack of exposure for minorities. Contrarily, most people of color were hired in the service component of my chosen career field. As a result of this unbalanced reality, I often found myself one of very few or sometimes the only person of color at the table during staff meetings, conferences, and professional development sessions. Rather than cowering or recoiling to this reality, I accepted it as a challenge. I knew that my performance and conduct would help shape the stereotypical reality for those who were observing me. Realistically, sometimes this reality grew tiresome. Perseverance and endurance had to kick in when my motivation began to waver. There was simply too much riding on my shoulders; my family's well-being, my career, and my team members were all depending on me.

I personally did not like being labeled by anyone. Labels bring up images of stereotyping—trying to place someone in a box. I was never fond of others attempting to place a label on me. I simply wanted to be treated as an individual. If you must judge me, judge me by how I interact with you, not by how others who may look like me interacted with you.

Playing the so-called race card at work can potentially be the beginning of the end of your career. During my grinding—steady and continuous employment days, many professional people of color knew this, including me. As a result of the potential severity of this issue, I had to be very selective about when, where, and how to unleash this proverbial genie out of the bottle. Even though covert racism was in existence almost daily over the course of my forty-year professional career, I never formally filed a racism or discrimination complaint with human resources or the EEOC. What I did do, however, was address my concerns at the lowest level possible. Fortunately for me, I was able to articulate my concerns in such a way that prevented me from having to elevate them to a formal level. I say this with the full knowledge that the path I took may not work for others.

Select Questionable and Controversial Experiences from My Four Decades of Employment

As you might imagine, there could be a lot to reveal, covering forty years of employment, with the potential of encountering racism lurking around every corner. When twenty years of service in the military and twenty years of employment for a local government are combined, plus five years of entrepreneurship, the number of discriminatory stories and incidents are numerous. Most workplace racism and prejudice are not overt. In fact, most of the incidents were covert, that is they were concealed or undercover. Recognizing covert racism and prejudice is a special talent or gift. I have witnessed others endure this covert racism and not recognize it for what it truly was. What is also noteworthy is that my experiences were spent in a career field where traditionally African Americans did not have widespread exposure.

Breaking down the forty years of employment, thirty-three of those years were spent in a supervisory or management capacity. There were several "I was the first African American" moments. It was not uncommon for me to sit at the table in staff meetings and look around to find there was no one else at the table who looked like me. Because of the overwhelming number of incidents during this lengthy timeframe, I have elected to share and present my encounters based on two categories. One, I am sharing my experiences in a manner that will prohibit compromising any one individual. Two, I am only sharing experiences that ate at my inner spirit. I discovered that your inner spirit, your internal radar, is where and when you know what you are feeling is real. Real racism is that feeling that causes your stomach to tie up into knots. This is when you know, without a doubt, that the uncomfortable feelings you are experiencing are confirmed. I have decided to share a few, select work-related incidents. The following incidents are wide-ranging in scope:

- Generally, over the course of my careers, I could place my managers and supervisors into one of two categories. One, I had managers and supervisors who welcomed educated, competent, and confident black males. They encouraged autonomy and proactive problem-solving, and they believed in minimal supervision. They were comfortable with telling you what they wanted or needed and allowed you to work through your tasks and assignments to achieve solutions. Two, I had managers and supervisors who were somehow threatened by those same attributes. They were obsessed with power, micromanaging, control, and loyalty, favoring *yes* men and cheerleaders. Most of the challenges I have encountered with managers and supervisors occurred when a new manager or supervisor arrived on the scene who fit into the second category described above. I was not motivated by fear. As a result of not being motivated by fear, my managers and supervisors who thrived on instilling fear and a demand for total blind loyalty usually encountered a somewhat contentious but professional relationship with me. I believed that if you were competent at your job, the loyalty issue would take care of itself.

o It became clear to me why so many males, minority men, struggle as they move up the so-called corporate ladder. It appears as if the higher you moved up in position and authority, the more you are expected to marginalize or turn a blind eye, in some situations, to your individuality, morals, core values, and integrity.

o I learned that you had to draw that proverbial line in the sand when it came to your morals, beliefs, and integrity. I also discovered there are many of all races who had no problem with violating or having to periodically compromise their personal attributes.

o During my second reenlistment in the army, I took a reenlistment option to return to Europe for a second time. I signed the contract and was approximately three months away from departing. My unit of assignment at the time received orders to send a contingent of personnel to the Sinai Peninsula (Middle East). My new commander, the rank of major, at the time decided he was going to divert me from my contractual reenlistment option and order me to report to the Sinai Peninsula. Without offering too much detail, this new commander had personal issues with me that were not related to my performance. Perhaps the extremely positive carryover accolades about me from his predecessor did not set well with him. Long story short, I requested an audience with the brigade commander who had the rank of colonel. The brigade commander was superior in rank to my commander. In the military, you don't go against the chain of command, and you certainly do not formally challenge a commissioned officer, particularly when you are a young noncommissioned officer, only six years in. After a surprisingly short meeting, the colonel ruled in my favor. I was in awe to even be standing in the office of a colonel. This was potentially a career-threatening decision, but I knew I was right. For the remainder of my three months, the major was extremely polite to me. Eventually, I would go on to meet my future wife as a result of the actions I had taken. Why me? Could another candidate have been identified? Why couldn't my commander have simply informed his superiors that he could not fill the request? Was he using me to advance his career and to support his "I can do anything I'm asked" leadership approach? Or was there something else?

o   I was working with an executive staff in a high-level position. I had been there for a year and had never experienced or received any type of work-related disciplinary action. One of my duties and responsibilities was to directly brief the commander who had the rank of colonel. In fact, my job title and responsibilities were the only ones of its kind on the entire military installation. A new supervisor (captain) came on board and made significant changes to include changing the briefing format where he personally briefed the commander. I did not react. Shortly thereafter, a friend with the rank of major advised me to seek another job within the organization. The major indicated that he thought the move would be in my best interest. Based on the major's recommendation and my instincts, I voluntarily accepted a less prestigious position to protect my career. Interestingly, no one ever asked why I decided to leave. It is not necessary for me to share the obvious.

o   As an operating unit manager, I had total autonomy of all day-to-day operational decisions. Generally, my managers were rarely available without appointment. It was common for customers to ask to speak to the person in charge when they were unhappy with a customer service-related issue coming from my operational business unit. Once it was determined that I was in charge, there was often bewilderment from customers who were asking for help. Astonishment was detected with the discovery of having the buck stop with me. Another way of putting it was it was common for some people to attempt to bypass me and circumvent who they could speak to.

o   In situations where shared passwords with executive team members was protocol to access certain systems, I was routinely provided a password that included the word "redneck." The owner(s) was quite comfortable with sharing such information.

o   In one memorable work-related incident, a formal complaint was filed by an employee. This particular employee did not like their annual evaluation. The evaluation was a below-standard evaluation. The employee opted for a hearing. I might add, opting for a hearing was well within their rights. During the course of the evaluated twelve months, the employee had twenty-one documented and signed write-ups. During the hearing process, the lawyer representing my business unit, my assistant, and the supervisor who administered the evaluation just happened to be African American. The employee and the hearing officer were white. The hearing officer opted to attack the validity of the evaluation itself. The hearing officer did not like the way the evaluation was written. Keep in mind that the same evaluation was used throughout the year for all other assigned coworkers/employees without concern or incident. In fact, the evaluation was approved by human resources. After a reset, lawful and logical minds prevailed; the actions and annual evaluation were validated. The thought of the hearing officer attempting to ignore the twenty-one write-ups and opting to focus on the validity of the written evaluation was mind-boggling to me. It was as if the hearing officer was digging deep to find a way out for the employee.

o   I had one of those very nice, high-quality floor-mounted globes on display in my office. Unintentionally, there were several instances when the African continent was displayed, facing the entrance or doorway. I started noticing that when one of my managers/supervisors would walk into my office, they would turn the globe, almost like a playful child, so that once the turn was completed, the African continent was no longer visible. Really! If this was an isolated incident, it would not be worth mentioning, but I tested the premonition I had. As a result of my hunch, I purposely positioned my globe this way on numerous occasions, and the manager's/supervisor's actions were the same. As I wasn't sure of what I was witnessing at the time, the level of pettiness blew me away. I never let my manager/supervisor know what I had discovered.

o   I was driving a company car to a meeting. During this particular trip, a small rock from a construction truck hit the windshield and placed a small chip in the window. After returning from my meeting and as a precautionary, I took a photo and reported this incident. According to policy, I was not required to report this incident because of the limited amount of monetary damage involved. Wouldn't you know it? After reporting this incident, human resources decided I should take a post incident drug test. When you consider the nature of the incident, the loss in production time to go take the drug test, the fact that I was a midlevel manager, and the cost involved in administering the test, was this a cost-effective and sensible decision? Then again, one must always ask, what was the motivation behind the decision to require me to have a drug test? At the time, I knew of no other peer who had a similar experience. Yes, I was the only African American midlevel manager at the time. Coincidently, estimated cost of repair was maybe sixty dollars.

o   As the only African American midlevel manager, I have been at the center of an executive-level debate concerning organizational realignment. So what was the source of the debate? The current manager/supervisor at the time argued for retaining me on their team. This current manager/supervisor and I had established a rapport and a good working relationship. I was offered autonomy and the opportunity to work for someone whom I respected. The opposing argument coming from the other manager/supervisor was that I needed to be under their supervision because I was offered too much freedom and needed to be reeled in. The only comment I'll make about the person who offered up the opposing argument was that this person was a known micromanager and was suspected of harboring feelings against employees who didn't look like him. This information was shared with me by someone who participated in this process.

o During the months leading up to the first election of President Barack Obama, I had numerous discussions about the pending election with my manager/supervisor. These discussions were initiated by my manager/supervisor. A particular discussion that stood out was one about the fear and belief that there would be a nationwide riot among African Americans if then US Senator Obama lost the presidential election. I jokingly responded that I had heard the same thing about supporters of US Senator Bob Dole if he had lost the election. You see, I understood that for many of my constituents, I may have been the only African American they knew, where they felt comfortable about bringing up such lightning rod issues. As you might imagine, this was very uncomfortable for me at work. Fast-forward to today, I currently have numerous friends and acquaintances who feel comfortable enough with our relationship to bring up controversial topics that they may not otherwise bring up with others. In fact, I think that having civil discussions with others who may vehemently oppose your point of view is encouraging and is a positive step. Keep in mind that having these type of discussions on a personal level is okay but the same does not apply while at work.

o I was deeply focused on being a top performer and subject matter expert. Because I was not a cheerleader or a *yes* man, I always knew that I had to perform on a level above average. Any misstep would be viewed as an opening to discredit. I decided to live with this reality versus having to live with the alternative. One very poignant example involved filing my travel reimbursement claim after returning from a business trip. The policy in effect at the time was all claims had to be completed within seventy-two hours upon return. I returned from a business trip after close of business on a Thursday. On the next day, Friday morning, after filing my claim, it was determined I owed the company $1.25 to fully settle my travel claim. At that time, only a check or money order was acceptable for reimbursement. Since I did not routinely carry a checkbook, I asked if the $1.25 check could be submitted on the following Monday. The response was yes. On Monday, as agreed, the $1.25 personal check was submitted. Six months later, upon submitting my request for another business travel request, I discovered I had been banned from business travel for one year. I was told that the official reason for the ban was I had failed to finalize my previous claim within the seventy-two-hour window. The irony of this decision was that I was not informed that this decision had been made, and I was not afforded an opportunity for rebuttal. I felt this decision was made deceitfully. I felt this decision was made as punishment rather than as a corrective action. After requesting a meeting to discuss this decision, the manager/supervisor volunteered to reverse the decision. I informed the manager/supervisor that I did not want them to fall on their sword for me, and if I decided to travel during the current budget year, I would prefer to pay out of pocket. It is important to note that I was not an entry-level employee, but in fact I was an operating unit manager in charge of a multimillion-dollar operating budget.

I have chosen to avoid discussing the deeply repugnant incidents. As you might imagine, there were additional incidents that I have elected not to mention due to their compromising nature and potential lawful ramifications. I do, however, want to provide a sampling of the incidents I had to endure.

While engaging other African American peers from other professional career fields, I discovered that the encounters I was experiencing were not isolated encounters. I have spoken with executives, bankers, engineers, police officers, fire fighters, pilots, educators, lawyers, and pharmacists. They all have had some head-scratching and mind-boggling experiences that they have had to overcome during their professional careers. Let me note, the peers I am referring to were top performers in their respective fields. These professionals had tenure, and they were subject matter experts, productive, and had no record of recurring disciplinary problems.

With every fiber in my body, in each and every situation, I tried to downplay the race and racism element. Only after going through the process of deduction would I even consider race as a factor. The process of deduction involved exploring all possibilities of why these incidents occurred. After having no logical explanation or justification, I had to conclude that other than race and/or racism, there was no other reason these incidents were occurring.

You may ask, why didn't I say or do something about some of the incidents? If you have not already, you will soon discover that you must pick and choose your battles very carefully. I elected to fight the strategic battles versus the mundane, everyday battles. Oftentimes this was an everyday ethical dilemma. Sometimes your reactions work best when subtle; on other occasions, you've got to decide when to turn it up a notch.

Are minority business professionals under more race and racism scrutiny than those who may work in other industries like the service industry, for example? Or are those who may work in a paraprofessional or service industry forced to undergo more discriminatory hardships and challenges? Or regardless of the industry or career field, do people of color simply catch more hell when we find ourselves in positions of authority and responsibility? Or regardless of career field, are we a target because some of us simply strive to operate in excellence? Can you be so competent that your competence combined with your color creates resentment? Can you project so much self-discipline and wit that this creates envy? I don't know the answers to these questions, but I would sure love to crack open that egg to find the real answer.

Companies and organizations who allow managers/supervisors to operate in a discriminatory manner all have some things in common. They are a powerful machinery. They have lots of money to mount any challenge you may be considering. And at all costs, the executives and management team will circle the wagons, and the team is expected to stick together, no matter the cost. I did not volunteer or work for a small business or organization until retirement, but I would imagine that discriminatory behavior and practices are more easily detected when they occur in smaller businesses or organizations.

How was I shaped and motivated by chapter five?

The workplace, for many of us, is perhaps the most challenging aspect of our daily lives, even without having to endure racism and injustice. If you add racism to this equation, the stress and anxiety levels intensify even more. Many feel trapped. You need your job. Each individual is different, and each situation is different; your actions and reactions are limitless. The key point is that the workplace during a lifetime is a marathon, not a sprint. Overcoming perceived prejudices on the job requires thoughtful strategy and responses, tolerance, compromise, training (knowing what to do), making proper assessments, knowing policies and procedures, and recognizing who to trust and not trust. All these attributes come into play when attempting to successfully navigate your way in, around, and through the workplace environment. One small misstep can destroy a lifetime worth of achievements. Know this: it does not matter what the vision or mission statement says; everybody is not treated the same.

Early in my career, I'm not sure when, I learned that I had to outperform my peers to achieve equal or greater recognition. I knew that my performance could possibly pave the way for others. As a supervisor and manager, I knew that I was constantly being monitored and evaluated. I knew that being mediocre or average meant failure. I knew that becoming complacent at anything was to be avoided at all costs. I also knew that any major misstep would be used against me and could potentially become a game changer to my career. Unbelievably, I found out that being too competent and confident actually worked against me on numerous occasions. At times, it was as if I had to tone it down a notch so that my supervisors would not feel insecure. Oddly, I welcomed all challenges.

Simply put, understanding these variables is how I was shaped and motivated by this chapter.

CHAPTER 6

Statistics Impacting Race and Racism

*For those who have seen the earth from space, and for the
hundreds and perhaps thousands more who will, the experience
most certainly changes your perspective. The things that we share
in our world are far more valuable than those which divide us.*
—Donald Williams

*Bigotry lives not just in our words but in our
actions, thoughts, and institutions.*
—DaShanne Stokes

I RECALL HAVING A CONVERSATION at the local cigar shop with a colleague who was white. Our discussion led to the question, what percentage of the U.S. population is black? He argued the percentage had to be somewhere around 30 percent. I shared with him that the actual figure was closer to 13 percent. Right then and there, I encouraged my colleague to research the facts. He was shocked. Two take-a-ways, 1.) My colleague's response was based on his perception of the urban population & not on the United States as a whole. 2.) The facts were accessible to him all along, yet he simply relied on what he thought, rather than the facts. This is just one small example of why it is so important to research facts rather than rely on assumptions or perceptions. This private conversation did not create any harm however, can you imagine the potential damage that could be inflicted by people of power and authority who make decisions and create policy while intentionally or unintentionally ignoring the facts?

The purpose of statistics: Statistics teaches people to use limited samples to make intelligent and accurate conclusions about a greater population. The use of tables, graphs, and charts plays a vital role in presenting the data being used to draw conclusions.

Data is real. I have discovered that if people are unaware of what data reveals, their interests in data analysis is marginalized at best.

There is a new narrative that has entered into mainstream society called "fake news." I am not sure who initiated this narrative, and I don't plan to spend a lot of research trying to determine the origins. The narrative is real. I know this to be true because within the last three years, I have had some very lively debates about the authenticity of *fake news.*

The only way to counter this narrative is via the truth, conversation based on acceptable and factual resources. If, by chance, acceptable and factual resources are rejected, the only choice that remains is to basically shut it down.

Reject information that is fed or forced into you by others. Try to become your own researcher. Statistics and data from reputable resources are the best alternative to so-called fake news. Are you disciplined or undisciplined? Are you informed or uninformed? Are you inquisitive or uninterested? Are you a leader or a follower? If you don't stand for something, you will fall for anything. Do not allow yourself to be indecisive about life-altering issues. Stand up. Be account-able. Educate yourself to be able to intelligently explain what you believe or what you feel. If you are unable to do so, you position yourself where others may reject you or question your position. Weigh or assess the contrasting issues against the facts and choices made, and take ownership of what you discover. In many instances, the answers we are searching for are clear; the problem is our denial of what we know to be true, even if the conclusions are different than what you initially thought they would be. Allow truth, facts, common sense, and rationale to guide you. This is the essence of what is conveyed when we say, "It's as plain as black and white." The problem expands when we attempt to skew what is known or truthful into a narrative that will benefit us rather than support what is true, just, fair, or impartial. We place our selfish desires over what is proven to be right and wrong.

In this chapter, I have chosen to examine some data that's detrimental to race relations in America, starting with the use of force by law enforcement agencies. There are huge racial disparities in how police use force. Black people are much more likely to be shot by police than their white peers.

An analysis of the available FBI data shown below found that US police kill black people at disproportionate rates. Black people accounted for 31 percent of police killing victims in 2012, even though they made up just 13 percent of the US population. Although the data is incomplete because it's based on voluntary reports from police agencies around the country, it highlights the vast disparities in how police use force.

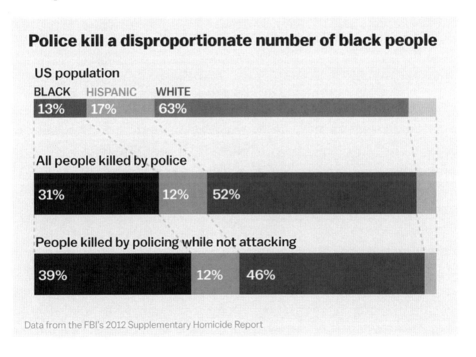

Police kill a disproportionate number of black people

US population

BLACK	HISPANIC	WHITE
13%	17%	63%

All people killed by police

31%	12%	52%

People killed by policing while not attacking

39%	12%	46%

Data from the FBI's 2012 Supplementary Homicide Report

The disparities appear to be even starker for unarmed suspects, according to an analysis of 2015 police killings by *The Guardian*. Racial minorities made up about 37.4 percent of the general population in the US and 46.6 percent of armed and unarmed victims, but they made up 62.7 percent of unarmed people killed by police.

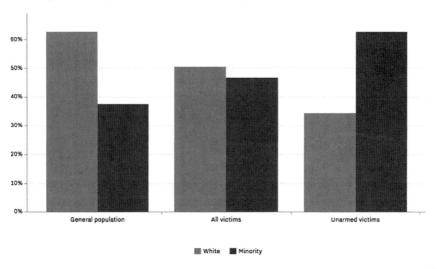

Unarmed victims of police killings are more likely to be minorities

Racial demographics in percent of general population in 2014 and people killed by police from January to May 2015

Source: The Guardian

Vox

These disparities in police use of force reflect more widespread racial inequities across the entire American criminal justice system. Black people are much more likely to be arrested for drugs even though they're not more likely to use or sell them. And black inmates make up a disproportionate amount of the prison population.

Unemployment rates: black vs. white

In February 2015, the US Bureau of Labor Statistics published a report wherein unemployment rates in the United States were addressed. According to the report, the unemployment rate for African Americans was 10.4 percent while the comparable rates for whites, Hispanics, and Asians were 4.7 percent, 6.6 percent, and 4.0 percent, respectively. This is while the national unemployment rate was 5.5 percent. Thus, the unemployment rate among blacks in the United States was almost twice as much than the national unemployment rate.

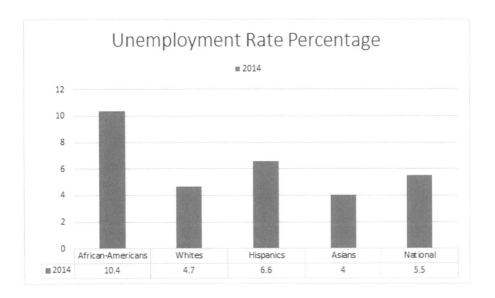

It should be noted that fewer job opportunities for members of the black community, in the United States, should not be attributed to lower education. In fact, the above-mentioned report by the US Bureau of Labor statistics also indicates that in 2014, 23.7 percent of unemployed blacks in the United States had attended some college, of whom 15.4 percent had bachelor's degrees, and 4.5 percent had advanced degrees.

A 2014 study by the Young Invincibles, a nonpartisan education and economic opportunity advocacy group, revealed that an African American college graduate has the same job prospects as a white high-school dropout or a white person with a prison record. The study attributed the gap to racial discrimination.

Arguably, high rates of unemployment in the black community have implications for a few other social problems, including violence and poverty, which will be addressed in the following sections.

Poverty and Income
According to the 2012 US Census Bureau American Community Survey (ACS), the poverty rate for Black Americans in the year 2012 was 28.1 percent, while this number was at 25.5 percent seven years before that, in 2005. The increase in poverty rate among African Americans between 2005 and 2012 was observed in

every demographic of African Americans, except those aged sixty-five and over, since they experienced a decrease from 21.2 percent to 19 percent. The highest rate of poverty was reported for black families with children under eighteen, headed by a single mother. Reportedly 47.5 percent of single-mother families lived in poverty, while this number was at only 8.4 percent for married-couple black families.

On the word of the ACS briefs for the years 2007–2011, 42.7 million people that make up 14.3 percent of the US population's income are below the poverty level.

The same report provides data on poverty by breaking down numbers by race. Accordingly, the highest national poverty rates were recorded for Native Americans and Alaskan Natives, with a 27.0 percent poverty rate, and second came the blacks or African Americans, which recorded a 25.8 percent poverty rate.

On account of the data collected by the US Census Bureau, which presents annual estimates of median household income and poverty by state, race, sex, and other smaller geographic units based on data collected in the ACS, median household income was $53,657 in 2014. The number does not show a statistically significant difference in real terms from the data reported in 2013 on median household income, which was recorded at $54,462.

The real average income of non-Hispanic, white households experienced a slight decline of 1.7 percent between the years 2013 and 2014, dropping from $61,317 to $60,256. For black, Asian, and Hispanic-origin households, however, the 2013–2014 changes in real average household income were insignificant and thus overlooked in the report.

As for the median income of the race groups, the highest was recorded for Asian households with an average income of $74,297 in the year 2014. The median income of non-Hispanic white households was $60,256 while for Hispanic households the median income was $42,491. Blacks or African Americans, once again, recorded the lowest earning, and their median income was recorded the lowest of all races, with $35,398 for the same year.

The official website of the United States Department of Labor, the Bureau of Labor Statistics published a report on "Median usual weekly earnings of full-time wage and salary workers by age, race, Hispanic or Latino ethnicity, and sex, fourth quarter 2015 averages, not seasonally adjusted," for the fourth quarter of the year 2015. The report, which was last modified on January 22, 2016, reveals that Asians had the highest average weekly income in the last quarter of the year 2015 and earned $1,178 on average, while Hispanic and Latino men and women in America recorded the lowest weekly income by earning $624 on average. Blacks or African Americans earned slightly more than Hispanic and Latinos and recorded median weekly earnings of $643. Black or African American men, however, earn even lower than Hispanic or Latinos and record the lowest median weekly earnings of full-time wage and salary workers, among men of all races, by making $674 per week.

Incarceration

The United States has the highest rate of incarceration and is the largest imprisoner of the world, holding 20 percent of the world's prison population, while the country's population makes up only 5 percent of the world's total population. Not only is the US population the largest in the world, the country has witnessed an enormous growth in its inmate population over the past thirty years. According to *The Sentencing Project*, the prison population of the United States was recorded at 2.2 million in the year 2013, which shows a 500 percent increase over the past thirty years.

The statistics show a 500 percent increase in US prison population, while the US population has just increased by 45 percent. According to the Bureau of Justice Statistics Prisoners Series, behind the scenes of the US prison industrial complex, you can find, "The political and economic interests of America's elite: laws; zealous prosecutors; the legislative, judicial, and executive branches at the local, state, and federal levels; the media; transnational corporations; schools; the church; the police; virtually every American institution; and the ideologies and rhetoric of racism, fear, and crime and punishment all work together to maintain the world's largest prison system."

The following chart provided by *The Sentencing Project* is based on data from the Bureau of Justice and shows the rapid growth in incarceration rates in the United States from 1925 to 2013. The chart does not consider the imprisonment rate at private prisons in the United States, a rate which is itself a unique one all across the globe.

U.S. State and Federal Prison Population, 1925-2013

One might contend that this hefty population of imprisoned people is mainly because they are real criminals who deserve to be kept in prisons; this is not the case. The number of inmates kept behind bars continues to rise tremendously while the crime rate reveals a downward trend. Despite the fact that violent crime has declined in the US, the incarceration rate has tripled since 1980. About thirteen million people are brought to American jails in any given year. It is totally absurd to mention that more than six million people are under *correctional supervision* in the US. These statistics are surprising, as one in fifty Americans has experienced prison sometime in their life either as an inmate or while on parole or probation. Currently, one out of every one hundred Americans is being imprisoned.

One of the most significant implications that mass incarceration has for the American society is that a large number of children will grow up in families where fathers are absent, and thus chances of poverty, low educational competences, higher rates of violence, and drug abuse, among many other issues, are much stronger.

Drug Policy Alliance published a report in June 2015 where the institute has raised concern over mass incarceration in America and the discriminate rates of imprisonment that have largely targeted people of color in the United States. According to the report, 2.7 million children are growing up in US households where at least one parent is incarcerated.

This is while on the word of the same report, two-thirds of these parents are jailed for nonviolent offenses. The situation is even worse for black or African American children. Reportedly, one in nine black children has an incarcerated parent, while this number stands at one in twenty-eight children for Latinos (a.k.a. Hispanics) and one in fifty-seven for white children.

The fact that a major proportion of these parents were jailed for nonviolent offenses has one significant implication that the article has been trying to shed light on, and that is racial discrimination in the American judicial system.

The rate of black incarcerations continued to record higher than all other races in the year 2014. The US Bureau of Justice Statistics published a report in September 2015 wherein it provides data on incarceration in the United States. On the section where the incarceration rate of the country is breaking down by race, the data shows that of all black male residents, 2.7 percent were serving at least one year in prison. Although the black community is experiencing the highest rate of incarceration, the situation is not far better for Hispanic males. According to the US Bureau of Justice Statistics, 1.1 percent of Hispanic males were serving sentences of at least one year in prison when the data was collected in 2014. This is while the rate of incarceration for White American males was less than 0.5 percent.

The report further adds that, according to the data collected on December 31, 2014, black males had higher imprisonment rates than prisoners of other races or Hispanic origin within every age group. The rate at which black males were incarcerated was 3.8–10.5 times greater at each age group than that of the white males and 1.4–3.1 times greater than rates for Hispanic males.

What exacerbates the situation for the black community and could have stern implications for black or African Americans is that the largest disparity happens for black men imprisoned as young as eighteen or nineteen. In fact, 1,072 per 100,000 black male residents aged eighteen to nineteen were imprisoned, which means black or African American males at this age are over ten times more likely to be in state or federal prison than whites. White Americans aged eighteen or nineteen were imprisoned at the rate of 102 per 100,000.

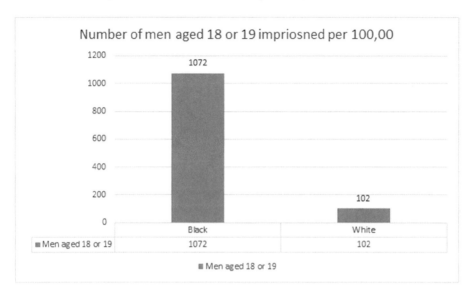

According to the Pew Research Center, the mass incarceration of young black males has stern long-term results and affects employment rate, percentage of families headed by single mothers, black-on-black violence, educational competences, and so on.

The highest total imprisonment rates by race and Hispanic origin were recorded for males ages thirty to thirty-four. According to the abovementioned report, 6,412 per 100,000 black males, 2,457 per 100,000 Hispanic males, and 1,111 per 100,000 white males were serving in prison in December 2014.

More than 1 percent of white male Americans aged thirty to thirty-nine were in state or federal prison by the end of the year in 2014. Black males of the same age group surpassed 6 percent of their total US population in prison.

Moreover, a significant disparity also existed between the incarceration rates for black women than for women of other races. Women ages thirty to thirty-four had the highest incarceration rates among blacks or African Americans with 264 per 100,000 black females of the same age in prison. This is while white women of the same age recorded 163 per 100,000, and Hispanic females were imprisoned at a rate of 174 per 100,000. Hence, black females were between 1.6 and 4.1 times more likely to be imprisoned than white females of any age group.

Racial gaps in household income persist

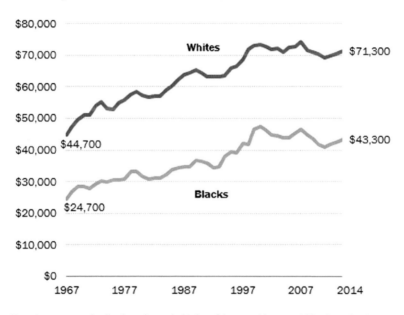

Racial gaps in household income persist

Median adjusted household income in 2014 dollars

Note: Income standardized to a household size of three and is reported for the calendar year prior to the survey year. For details, see Methodology. Race and ethnicity are based upon the race and ethnicity of the head of household. Whites and blacks include only those who reported a single race. Data from 1970 to 2014 include only non-Hispanic whites and blacks; data prior to 1970 include Hispanics.
Source: Pew Research Center tabulations of the 1968-2015 Current Population Survey Annual Social and Economic Supplement (IPUMS)
"On Views of Race and Inequality, Blacks and Whites are Worlds Apart"

PEW RESEARCH CENTER

How was I shaped and motivated by chapter six?
Discussions about race and racism are often challenged or disputed because of a lack of exposure to facts, denial, lack of education, untruths, and a preference by

others to secure economic, political, and financial advantages (power). To many of us, having to defend the realities of race and racism is a tireless endeavor. Those of us who are recipients of this terrible epidemic know our experiences are real without having to endure the burden of proof. Oftentimes, the only method to challenge such claims is through statistics and hard facts. The undisputed theme behind chapter six is, with credible data and facts, opposing viewpoints are difficult to dispute.

Most men would rather deny a hard truth than face it.
—George R. R. Martin

CHAPTER 7

How Did We Get to Where We Are? Why Aren't We Doing More?

—⟆—

We must be the change we wish to see in the world.
—Mahatma Gandhi

—⟆—

FROM SLAVERY TO THE EMANCIPATION Proclamation, to the Civil Rights Movement, to the election of Barack Obama, has the playing field for people of color and minorities ever been equal? If not, when will the day come for total equality? President Abraham Lincoln formally issued the Emancipation Proclamation on January 1, 1863, African Americans have been waiting 157 years.

Perhaps the answer to the questions of how we got to where we are and why aren't we doing more is linked to our history, our ancestors, our upbringing, and our individual visionary outlook for justice and equality for all. The link includes what is passed down from one generation to the next. Our attitudes, traditions, learned behaviors, teachings, values, ethics, and ideas can definitely be passed from one generation to the next. You may see progress on the surface; however, progress or a lack of progress is oftentimes deeply imbedded in the hearts of men. In other words, some progress has been achieved outwardly, but the hearts of men remain unchanged. Outwardly, change is visible, but inwardly things remain the same. What are some of those heart-related realities that may have impacted how we got to where we are today?

- Hate
- Fear
- Apathy
- Complacency
- Oppression
- Lack of opportunity
- Quest for power
- Hopelessness
- Protectionism
- The love of money
- Feelings of superiority or inferiority

Almost every single day, when you turn on the local or national news, you will encounter stories of injustices committed against people of color and other minorities. Have you ever paused and asked, as a country and as a people, how did we get to where we are today? Truth be told, we have a well-documented and unfortunate history.

I want to briefly examine several race massacres or riots that devastated black America. Perhaps by identifying some of America's demoralizing history, some insight may be offered into how we got to where we are.

1. **Colfax, Louisiana, 1873.** The Colfax massacre occurred on Easter Sunday, April 13, 1873, in Colfax, Louisiana—the seat of Grant Parish—where approximately 150 black men were murdered by white Southerners who had formed a militia. Three white men died in the confrontation, with at least one said to have been shot by his own side. The cause of the massacre was the disputed gubernatorial contest in 1872 between Republicans and Democrats.

2. **Wilmington, North Carolina, 1898.** Wilmington, North Carolina, was a thriving area with a majority black population. There were also several black elected public officials, forcing whites to share power. By the

election of 1898, black men were prevented from voting to push out the black elected officials. However, white supremacists could not stop the economic power that blacks had already created. Therefore, they destroyed black Wilmington with terrorism.

The day after the 1898 election, whites announced the "white declaration of independence." They overthrew the Wilmington government, destroyed the printing press, and forced out the mayor, and a mob of white men attacked black residents.

There were reportedly sixty to three hundred black people killed by domestic terrorism.

3. **Atlanta Massacre of 1906.** Like many race massacres, the violence in Atlanta at the turn of the century began with white women accusing black men of rape. On September 22, 1906, Atlanta newspapers reported that four white women alleged they were assaulted by black men, a claim that was completely unfounded. In reality, whites were threatened by upwardly mobile black communities in Atlanta, which they believed were taking away their jobs. This bogus report of sexual assault drove as many as two thousand white men to the streets, and they went into black communities to beat, stab, and shoot any black people in sight.

Communities were destroyed, and the unofficial death toll was up to one hundred people.

4. **Elaine, Arkansas, massacre, 1919.** Blacks outnumbered whites ten to one and were demanding economic justice, as many of them were forced into sharecropping. A union was created to protect sharecroppers, and whites were outraged at even the smallest move toward equality. In September of 1919, there was a union meeting among black workers, and whites showed up to riot. As a result, one white man was shot and killed. Whites convinced themselves there was a threat of a *black insurrection* and as usual reacted with violence. Hundreds of white men attacked black residents, but many fought back, including black veterans. Sadly, there were reports that over two hundred black people, including children, were killed.

Many who weren't killed were arrested and tortured while in custody. They were forced to *confess* about an insurrection with twelve men receiving the death penalty. They eventually became known as the Elaine

Twelve. With the help of the National Association for the Advancement of Colored People (NAACP), their case went to the US Supreme Court in 1923, and they were exonerated. This was one of the first times the NAACP won a case in front of the Supreme Court.

5. **Tulsa, Oklahoma, 1921.** The Tulsa race riot—also called the Tulsa massacre, Greenwood Massacre, or the Black Wall Street Massacre—of 1921 took place on May 31 and June 1, 1921, when mobs of white residents attacked black residents and businesses of the Greenwood district in Tulsa, Oklahoma. It has been called "the single worst incident of racial violence in American history." The attack, carried out on the ground and from private aircraft, destroyed more than thirty-five-square blocks of the district, the wealthiest black community in the United States at that time, known as Black Wall Street.

More than eight hundred people were admitted to hospitals, and more than six thousand black residents were arrested and detained, many for several days. The Oklahoma Vital Records Division officially recorded thirty-six dead. A 2001 state commission examination of events noted estimations from between thirty-six and three hundred killed in the rioting. And based on contemporary autopsy reports and death certificates, the commission confirmed thirty-nine black males, thirteen white males, and four unidentifiable bodies.

The riot began over Memorial Day weekend after a nineteen-year-old black shoe-shiner was accused of assaulting a seventeen-year-old white elevator operator. A subsequent gathering of angry local whites outside the courthouse where the man was being held, and the spread of rumors he had been lynched, alarmed the local black population, some of whom arrived at the courthouse armed. Shots were fired, and twelve people were killed—ten white and two black. As news of these deaths spread throughout the city, mob violence exploded. White rioters rampaged through the black neighborhood that night and morning, killing men and burning and looting stores and homes. Only around noon the next day the Oklahoma National Guard troops managed to get control of the situation by declaring martial law. About ten thousand black people were left homeless, and property damage amounted to more than $1.5

million in real estate and $750,000 in personal property—equivalent to $32.25 million in 2019.

6. **Rosewood, Florida, massacre, 1923.** A black community was burned to the ground after a white woman claimed she was assaulted by a black man on January 1, 1923. The first person killed was Sam Carter, a local blacksmith. He was tortured, and his mutilated body was hung from a tree. Sam Carter was one of many. There are reports that up to 150 black people were killed in Rosewood, Florida.

   After Rosewood was destroyed, a grand jury and special prosecutor decided there was not enough evidence for prosecution of the white men who killed innocent American citizens.

7. **Marianna riots, 1934.** Claude Neal was a twenty-three-year-old African American farmhand who was arrested in Jackson County, Florida, on October 19, 1934, for allegedly raping and killing a white woman.

   The body of Claude Neal was hung from a tree outside of the county courthouse. Photographers took souvenir photos of the body. When the sheriff discovered Neal's body, he cut it down and buried the man. A mob formed outside the courthouse, with over two thousand people having arrived by noon, but they were too late to see Neal's body. Some purchased picture postcards of the corpse from photographers for fifty cents each. The mob demanded that the sheriff hang Neal's body again outside the courthouse, but he refused.

   The whites started to riot. They attacked blacks that day, October 27, 1934, injuring about two hundred people caught on the street. The mob also attacked and injured two police officers among those trying to suppress the disorder. Some white people took great risks by protecting black people during the riots, often aiding people who worked for them. The mob headed into black areas of town, looting and burning houses. The governor of Florida called out 129 troops of the Florida National Guard, which managed to suppress the riots.

As I study these horrific events in our history, I am forced to ask, why? I believe there is a link between the *why* and the common denominators found in these historical events. As I see them, the common denominators include:

- Political oppression
- Fear
- Injustice
- Discrimination
- The enforcement of white privilege

Ironically, four of these incidents occurred in the twentieth century. Here we are today in the twenty-first century, ninety-seven years removed from the last race massacre, and we are still struggling with similar, ugly issues of our past. What impact does such historical incidents have on the psyche of the oppressed and oppressor? What impact does such incidents have on the psyche of a nation?

Many before us have paid a dear price, often with their lives. The notion that we casually cast aside the sacrifices of our ancestors is mind-boggling to me. Going forward, the only way this unfortunate history will change course is if we try to understand the past and force change through our actions as a result of our understanding.

How can we counter racism if we do not know how to adequately counteract it or its root causes and effects? Is the ability to recognize, accept, or counteract racism inherited? That is, did we develop our present day attitudes from our parents or ancestors? Was recognition or awareness handed down from one generation to the next? Can someone be raised in a way that would sharpen their ability to recognize and detect subtle or covert actions committed toward them? I truthfully do not know the answer, but what I do know is, time and time again, I have observed and encountered others who harbor deep rooted feelings about race and racism.

In terms of the ability to effectively recognize and counteract racism, I think it is the combination of many things. Most importantly, awareness starts at home. Do we raise our children to properly deal with diversity, racial insensitivities, justice, fairness, and truth? These attributes are the cornerstone and foundation to developing productive, future members of society. Certainly, as a result of our global society, our children and future generations must be able to successfully deal with diversity. Having to deal with diversity is simply unavoidable. If you are not equipped to adequately handle diversity in the workplace, at institutions of higher learning, or in the military, it will not take long for others to detect your inability to deal with these challenges. You may think your inabilities are well camouflaged; however, people can be vicious. Those who practice taking advantage of others are sure to attempt to size you up first before they engage. Aside from that, people are too sophisticated and educated to continue to be marginalized. Technology is so prevalent in our society. Social media and technology have proven to be a major deterrent as well as an enabler.

As we strive to do more, today, we continue to celebrate many African American firsts. The first African American to achieve this, the first African American to achieve that. Even though I have been placed in positions to be a trailblazer of sorts, at least four times in my life, I find myself somewhat conflicted with this reality. There are two schools of thought. One, the thought process for many is we must begin achievement at some place, so whenever or wherever that achievement happens to be, simply enjoy the hard-earned and long-overdue success. Many would argue that incremental progress is better than no progress. I get that. But secondly, this is now 2020, so why are we even having to celebrate being the first when so many years of so-called freedom and equality have already been celebrated? To the contrary, the long-delayed achievements can be viewed as something of sadness and disappointment. Some would argue the progress is too slow and, as a result, is a source of disappointment. It doesn't matter which side you are on; this is our current reality. The pace of progress is a source of pride for many while it is a source of frustration for many others.

Earlier, I mentioned how growth and maturity typically propel us toward a higher evaluation of self. That never-ending search for purpose can lead you toward the top of what is known as Maslow's hierarchy of self-actualization. That is the endless search for realizing personal potential, self-fulfillment, seeking personal growth, and peak experiences. There is a desire "to become everything one is capable of becoming." Why am I here? What is my purpose? Who am I? Where am I going? What do I want to achieve?

What can each individual do to respond to the question of why aren't we doing more? Below, I have provided some options:

- Grass roots involvement
    - Community engagement—helping children and the elderly
    - Participating in political forums and voting, supporting local candidates of choice

- o Supporting a local church
- o Attending town hall meetings
- Family
  - o Accountable and responsible parenting
  - o Mentoring and role modeling
  - o Teaching budgeting, financial responsibility, and proper decision-making
  - o Being accountable and responsible
- Education
  - o School board meeting participation
  - o Parent-teacher organization participation
  - o Career day at schools
  - o Volunteering for parent involvement with extracurricular activities
  - o Preparing to invest or guide your children's educational choices
  - o Encouraging some type of education beyond the high school level
    - College enrollment
    - Trade or technical school
    - Certification
    - Military
    - Stable employment
  - o Please note: The educational process never ends. It doesn't matter how educated you are or how old you are; reading, self-improvement, and self-empowerment lead to true self-fulfillment.
- Networking with others where there is a shared interest
- Investing/Fiduciary Responsibility
  - o 401(k)/501(k)
  - o Medical/dental/Life insurance
  - o Savings
  - o Minimize or eliminate debt
  - o Get a financial advisor
  - o Maintain an above average credit score
- Don't avoid jury duty; your participation could be a game changer for others
- Applying for grand juries where applicable

- Entrepreneurship—investing in yourself
- Giving time and money to worthy organizations and foundations
- Reading—self-empowerment
- Supporting organizations that promote justice and equality

Working with community members to solve problems is widely seen as one of the most effective tactics to help blacks achieve equality.

The Impact of Voting

Admittedly, as a young adult, I did not understand the significance of voting. I, too, was one of many who felt as if my vote would not make a difference. Times have changed; I have changed. What brought about the change? The change can be attributed to multiple reasons: maturity, life's experiences, world events, better understanding of the impact and process, education, access to technology, and even history.

Voting today is simply too important to ignore. Justifiably, politicians will ignore your issues and concerns if you are not engaged in the process. Your *no* vote is a vote for others who may oppose how you think and feel. Your *no* vote empowers your opponent; this is about as basic as it gets. It appears that people of color are only motivated when there is a crisis or when our backs are against the wall. Sadly, I also believe that many of us are intimidated by the voting process. Many of us simply do not want others to know what we don't know. As a result of political analytics, your opponent knows more about your voting or nonvoting patterns than you do. Ignorance is no longer an excuse.

Voting cannot change the past, but it can certainly impact the present and the future. Speaking of the future, whether we accept it or not, we owe a great deal to past and future generations. We owe past generations because of what they had to endure for us to enjoy many of the successes we experience today. We owe future generations because our current actions or inactions will be inherited by our children. Not only that, when your children follow your example, they would have been taught a very valuable lesson about the need to be heard and properly represented. This in-house education includes lessons on accountability and accepting civic responsibility. Caution: Do not rely on the school system to teach your children what you should have taught them.

While national elections are important for the nation as a whole, local elections are just as important. How does school board redistricting impact your child's education? Who decides what curriculum your child will be exposed to in school? How will local judgeships impact your community? Did I mention the importance of those who oversee the juvenile justice system? Is funding by the city council being considered or distributed to improve your community or neighborhood?

The national elections of the 44th and 45th Presidents offer us perhaps the biggest contrast ever in political ideology. This contrast has nothing to do with the color of each man's skin but has everything to do with their visions for all Americans. In the past, I did not have a fondness for the political process, but citizens of our great country can no longer afford to sit idle as others create policies that do not represent our best interest.

Voting is one way for you to take destiny into your own hands. Voting is empowerment. Voting ensures that those who may have neglected you in the past can no longer afford to continue the practices that they have so boldly pursued. I challenge each and every reader to get involved in the political process. If you haven't done so in the past, today is a good day to start.

Please note I did not say vote Democrat, Republican, or Independent. I am simply encouraging you to involve yourself in the process. Whoever gains your vote must earn it and represent your best interest.

After the 2018 midterm elections, even with the gains for people of color, I heard many say they were tired. They were tired of politics, voter suppression, injustice at polling locations, and outright division and hatred. I understand these feelings. I often felt this way as I was in the midst of working my way through two careers. My thought process was no matter how discouraging the political process may appear, it is critical to remain relevant and engaged. When you listen to the inner voices of right versus wrong, you must remain driven. At the end of the day, you've got to go home and look at the man or woman in the mirror. As I reflect, our ancestors had to endure unfathomable hardships, but through it all, they never gave up.

When I began this project, I experienced a self-conviction. I had been quietly fighting the racism and respect battle for a long time. All my fighting has been private, one-on-one, situational, and focused on fairness inside of the workplace.

It occurred to me that there is also an ongoing collective battle that is raging. This collective battle that I am referring to is the exact opposite of the private, one-on-one, situational, and fairness in the workplace related encounters. This collective battle is the battle of joining forces with others who endure frontline issues daily. I am talking about organizations that combine their collective resources together to confront racial injustice and inequality for the greater need. I am talking about organizations such as the Southern Poverty Law Center, UnidosUS (formerly National Council of La Raza), and American Civil Liberties Union. And of course, there are the traditional organizations such as the National Urban League, NAACP, Southern Christian Leadership Conference, and other similar organizations. I have discovered there are two unfortunate realities about these organizations. The first reality is people of color and minorities tend to not offer their support or seek help until they are confronted with a crisis situation. The second reality is many who have opposing viewpoints have attempted to radicalize these organizations. I don't see any of these organizations spewing hate, but I do see them pursuing justice and equality. While we are here, I do not condone violence unless I am placed in a compromising position where I have to physically defend my family or myself.

How was I shaped and motivated by chapter seven?
Studying history is important because it allows us to understand our past, which in turn allow us to understand our present. Studying our past can provide us with insight into our cultures of origin as well as cultures with which we might be less familiar, thereby increasing cross-cultural awareness and understanding.

What more can we do? We can:

- Understand our history that has contributed to racism and bigotry
- Get involved in grass roots issues
- Reinforce family values
- Place emphasis on education
- Focus on financial security and independence
- Accept civic responsibilities
- Focus on self-improvement and empowerment

As previously stated, race and racism are two of the most complex issues of our time. How did we get to where we are? The answer is complex and requires an examination of the events, politics, and policies of the past. Why aren't we doing more? To understand the thoughts behind why aren't we doing more requires each of us to do a self-assessment of how our individual actions or lack of action support or contribute towards the overall greater good. Look for, support, and participate in impactful core issues that will help to eradicate or reduce the cancerous effects of racism as it eats away at our society. If you are a parent, mentor, or person in a position of responsibility, you are modeling behavior for future generations. I cannot overemphasize how critical leading by example is. Most importantly, what you fail to teach your children at home will most certainly be taught by others outside of the home.

My motivation for sharing chapter seven is to present open and honest dialogue to help examine the enormous and complex problems associated with racial injustice, hatred, and bigotry. There is always hope.

CHAPTER 8

The Modern-Day Battlefield

*The scars and stains of racism are still deeply
embedded in the American society.*
—John Lewis

*Every time we turn our heads the other way when we see the
law flouted, when we tolerate what we know to be wrong,
when we close our eyes and ears to the corrupt because we
are too busy or too frighten, when we fail to speak out, we
strike a blow against freedom and decency and justice..*
—Robert F. Kennedy

SO HERE'S THE REALITY. PEOPLE of color in America can expect to have a hard time finding a job and be paid less for it when we do get it. We can expect to have a harder time getting a loan and pay a higher price when we do. Black and brown people can expect to have a harder time finding an apartment or a house, which may make it more likely that we end up in a *bad neighborhood*, which in turn may increase the risk of our children becoming involved with gangs, reduce our access to investment, reduce the quality of our children's education, and disadvantage us in a myriad of other ways. People of color can expect to be viewed and treated as a potential threat when we enter a grocery store, hail a taxi, or even move into a neighborhood. We can expect to have a hard time getting accepted to college, struggle to make the same grades and receive the same treatment from professors and advisors once we're there, and have a harder time graduating. Black and brown people can expect to be regularly pulled over or stopped while driving down the street—for no reason whatsoever—and when we do, we can reasonably fear that an officer with an attitude problem might arrest us on bogus charges or maybe even plant evidence on us. African Americans can expect police officers to operate under the assumption that we are guilty, and we can expect to be railroaded by the justice system—even to the point of being forced to take guilty pleas when we are innocent. If we were born in poverty, as a much larger percentage of us are than whites, we can reasonably expect to remain in poverty for our entire lives. We have very little reason to believe the American dream applies to us.

And that's when we're doing our best to do everything right! God forbid we should make a mistake, as many of us do, especially when we're young. If we do, we can expect to pay for it in ways that white people don't—often for the rest of our lives. People of color can expect to be treated as young criminals by our teachers and given harsher sentences—longer suspensions and quicker expulsions, both of which remove us from school and expose us to the gang element in some of our neighborhoods. Black and brown people can expect to be arrested, charged, convicted, and imprisoned for offenses that a large percentage of whites consider part of being a teenager or a college student. We can expect stiffer charges, higher conviction rates, and longer sentences.

And yes, black and brown mothers and fathers can reasonably fear that any time their child walks out the door, they might get in trouble with the law, get arrested, have their entire future ruined, or even, yes, be shot and killed by a police officer for no valid reason. And when that happens, they can expect that justice will not be served.

As we reflect on American history, all the way back to the Thirteenth Amendment, there were some elements of American history that were dark and dire with in-your-face aggression regarding Jim Crow laws. Here we are, over 140 years later, continuing on the path of enduring dark, dire, and in-your-face aggressive-type laws that disenfranchise law-abiding citizens. Examples include what is currently happening with voter suppression laws that impacted the 2018 midterm elections. I have selected four of the more recent and notorious voter suppression laws/incidents:

- Dodge City, Kansas. A suit alleging one polling location for thirteen thousand citizens that one polling location was moved outside the city limits prior to the 2018 midterm elections. By the way, the population of Dodge City is 70 percent Hispanic. US court ruled this law was enacted too close to the upcoming election to intervene.

- Waller County, Texas. Allegedly, a suit by Prairie View A&M students says the county was violating the students' rights by not setting up a voting site on the historically black campus—or in the city of Prairie View—during the first week of early voting. Meanwhile, voters in the city of Waller, which has a majority white population and half of the eligible voting age population of Prairie View, will have access to two early voting sites during the first week of early voting. Both of those sites were also scheduled to be open on Saturday. A polling site will also be open in the city of Waller during the second week of early voting. A pending compromise was offered by the county; results were pending.

- The state of Georgia. The Associated Press reported that fifty-three thousand voter registrations, 70 percent of them from black applicants, were being held by the secretary of elections office for failing to clear an "exact match" process that compares registration information to social security and state driver records. If the information does not match, often due to inconsistencies like a misspelled name, a middle name not being fully written out, or a missing hyphen, an application is held for additional screening, and the applicant is notified and given a period to correct their information. Data shows that many of these blocked voter registrations came from urban areas with high black populations. In areas with smaller black populations, the percentage of pending registrations from black voters often exceeds the percentage of black residents living in the area. In the eleventh hour, US courts ruled against Georgia voter suppression law.

- North Dakota. In addition to a strict ID requirement, the law requires all voters to provide proof of a residential street address—something many Native Americans who live on reservations simply do not have. Large numbers of Native Americans use post office boxes to receive mail and live on unmarked and unsigned streets. Many others live with various family members. Still, others have no idea that their streets even have names. In total, about five thousand Native Americans lack the required voter ID—larger than the electoral margin in 2016.

According to the Brennan Center for Justice, twenty-four states, predominantly controlled by Republicans, have enacted new voting restrictions since 2010: thirteen states have more restrictive voter ID laws in place, and six states have strict photo ID requirements; eleven have laws making it harder for citizens to register; seven cut back on early voting opportunities; and three made it harder to restore voting rights for people with past criminal convictions.

Politics and Racism

Politics in life are unavoidable. Politics permeates all segments of society. The way politics has influenced and perpetuated racism is real—this is my belief. Particularly, politics involving racism is front and center in our everyday lives. I believe that power, privilege, and money are the root cornerstones to racism in politics. Even if you are not into politics, understanding the impact politics has on racism is essential to how successful you are with moving forward with life, liberty, and happiness.

In the case of this book, I am describing politics as the ability to influence, manipulate, have power over, oppress, and control for the purpose of financial gain and/or influence. Understanding this reality is a form of everyday survival. Simply, if someone is attempting to take advantage of you, an understanding of what they are attempting to do is essential to your well-being. Recognition, educational awareness, and having an individual strategy are paramount.

During my life, I chose to focus on engagement as a way to overcome this reality. What do I mean by engagement? Engagement involves reading, listening, and contemplating one's own action. I have tried to control those things in life that I can control. I have control over my conduct, attitude, behavior, and my outlook on life. I have tried to be a leader and not a follower. Minimize excuses, maximize effort.

I have rebuffed racism from the inside out. What do I mean? Whatever positions I have been blessed with, I have tried to use those positions to my advantage as well as to the extent of helping others and helping other causes for the greater good. This was achieved by exercising self-discipline, role modeling, and setting standards that made it difficult for those in power to discriminate.

Current-day national politics speaks for itself; divisiveness, discriminatory laws, roll back of previous gains, and the non-diversity seen in political figures at the national level are clear evidence. There is a preference for political party versus the needs of all Americans. Ironically, the same observations noted at the national level can also be witnessed at the state and local levels.

Politicians cater to their constituents. Constituents are described as supporters of elected politicians. If you fail to exercise the power of the vote, your politicians will in turn fail to be an advocate for your issues and concerns. You essentially minimize your voice by your failure to engage. Not only that, your non-vote is in fact a vote for those who may oppose your values, issues, and concerns.

Your vote is a check and balance on those who are in power. Your vote is simply your voice. Without your vote, you are voiceless.

I have listed, in order, what I think are the primary issues of the modern-day battlefield:

1. A breakdown of the family unit
2. Employment discrimination
3. Flawed criminal justice system and law and order
4. Methods of voter suppression
5. Admissions/qualifications at institutions of higher learning
6. Health care/medical insurance access
7. Media/social media/technology/entertainment industry impact

Breakdown of the Family Unit

Parenting should be intentional. Failure in parenting can have a lifelong negative impact on you, your children, and your family. What exactly is being taught in the homes of people of color? What is being taught in the homes of Anglo Americans? Right versus wrong? Integrity? Respect for all mankind? Moral character? Fairness? Love? Hard work pays off? Be considerate of others? Empathy? Or is the opposite being taught? If societal, modern-day trends are any indication, I think we may know the answer. To what degree does our parenting failures contribute toward what many feel is an overall moral decline in society?

Once our children leave home, no matter how much we may wish to do so, we cannot create a protective bubble for them. Is it necessary to teach your male son how to act if or when he is stopped by law enforcement? They must be equipped to deal with diversity and adversity on their own. Building relationships, compromising, synergy, leading, and communicating are attributes that will be on full display once they enter into modern-day society.

Though somewhat callous, whatever you fail to teach your children, society will not hesitate to take up your slack.

Employment Discrimination

How does employment discrimination contribute toward racial bias? Less pay for people of color or having to deal with pay inequity, hiring discrimination, last hired/first fired, and discriminatory promotion practices are real, relevant, and verifiable by statistics. To say these issues do not exist is equivalent to turning a blind eye to reality. Can you imagine trying to provide for your family while having to face these types of issues? For many, this is a daily concern. As I reflect on my own experiences, these confrontations can have a *wear-you-down* effect that may sometimes lead you to a feeling of complete exasperation.

Not only that, but for many of us, our self-worth and self-value are tied to our ability to provide and support our families. When the ability to make a living is thwarted, minimized, or nonexistent, oftentimes a feeling of despair sets in. This hopelessness can lead some to desperation and illegal entrepreneurship.

Flawed Criminal Justice System/Law and Order

According to the data, the number of black males questionably killed by the law enforcement across this great country of ours has been alarming. As a follow-up to this alarming factoid, have you ever wondered why the same epidemic does not exist for black law enforcement officers encountering and questionably killing Anglo Americans at the same rate? I can only speculate why. Perhaps when Anglo American law enforcement officers say they fear for their lives, they actually mean it. They actually mean it because of racial stereotyping, fear, racial bias, and inadequate training and education.

Statistics disproportionately show how people of color are impacted by the criminal justice system. Do people of color, particularly African Americans, commit a majority of the crimes when African Americans make up only 13 percent of the US population? As indicated in chapter six, America's prisons and jails are overcrowded with people of color. If the head of household is a male who is incarcerated, who is left to provide, protect, and lead the family unit? What role does the privatization of the prison system play on law enforcement in ensuring there is a steady flow of clients to fill these enterprises?

I want to dedicate a little time to talk about the jury-selection process in America, particularly how all-white juries impact the prosecution of black men. It is mind-boggling to me that this practice is even deemed acceptable in modern-day society. I am not a legal expert, but I simply cannot conceive how anyone could label the fair prosecution of anyone by a jury comprised of all white or all black—when the accused is of the opposite race—as fair and impartial.

Racial discrimination in jury selection has a long history in the United States. It is specifically prohibited by law, which has been defined through a series of judicial decisions; however, juries composed solely of one racial group are legal in the United States.

Study after study has shown that all-white juries are harsher on black defendants, make more errors, and discuss fewer of the case facts. And all-white juries have historically been problematic, but they also aren't a thing of the past. As you might imagine, during my research, I found no evidence of an all-black jury ever convicting a white defendant. Why is that?

In the jury-selection process called "voir dire," potential jurors are questioned, and lawyers can dismiss jurors with cause for bias. But each side is also allowed to strike a certain number of jurors without giving a reason—these are called "peremptory challenges." This is where racial discrimination in jury selection becomes tricky.

The right to a jury trial is a hallmark of the American criminal justice system, and defendants generally have the right to be tried by a jury of their peers.

However noble the idea might be in theory, many legal experts acknowledge that, due to systemic racism, having a jury of your peers is often just an illusion. For African Americans, systemic racism in the criminal justice system has greatly contributed to mass incarceration, partly because blacks are more likely to be profiled, pulled over by police, searched, and arrested, according to legal experts. Once arrested, African Americans also are more likely to be detained prior to their hearing, which could take months.

Throughout the country, African Americans are overrepresented in felony convictions and therefore are more likely to be excluded from jury pools because an individual cannot serve as a juror if they've been convicted of a felony.

More than 80 percent of those charged with felonies are indigent. As a result, they are unable to hire an attorney and instead rely on representation by a public defender.

Currently, it's estimated that more than 75 percent of criminal cases use the public defense system. This means only one-quarter of Americans accused of a crime can afford or care to hire a private defense attorney. Of these citizens using the public defense systems, racial minorities constitute the vast majority.

I am not sure if anything can be done about this disparity in our criminal justice system. Reform? It's easy for some to simply say to avoid placing yourself in these situations, but our reality is sometimes these situations are simply unavoidable. After avoidance, there is education, wise lifestyle choices, and access to adequate resources. Can you change the hearts of man? It saddens me that I cannot offer more to this harsh reality.

Methods of Voter Suppression

What does voter suppression mean? Voter suppression is a strategy to influence the outcome of an election by discouraging or preventing specific groups of people from voting. Methods of voter suppression include the following:

- Impediments to voter registration
- Photo ID laws
- Purging of voter rolls
- Limitations on early voting
- Felon disenfranchisement
- Transgender disenfranchisement
- Disinformation about voting procedures
- Inequality in Election Day resources
- Gerrymandering

What is redistricting?

Members of Congress, state legislators, and many county and municipal offices are elected by voters grouped into districts. At least once per decade, usually after a census, district lines are redrawn, block by block. Populations change. Some districts gain residents; some lose them. Some districts increase the number of minorities; some districts lose them. District boundaries are redrawn to ensure each district has about the same number of people and to fulfill the constitutional guarantee that each voter has an equal say. Based on the 2010 census, each congressional district has an average population of about 711,000, which is nearly a 10 percent increase from the 2000 census, when each district had an average of 647,000 people. In 2010, some states lost congressional seats, and others gained them—for example, Texas gained four districts, and New York lost two.

Who draws the lines?

Each state decides. In most states, the line drawers are politicians along with hired consultants. Often, state legislators draw the map, which the governor can veto. Some states have special commissions that advise legislators on drawing the map or that serve as backup mapmakers if the legislature deadlocks. A few states have independent commissions, so politicians and public officials cannot directly draw their own districts. Some states try to prevent a single political party from controlling the process. Some do not, providing one party a major advantage if it controls the state legislature. In other states, politicians from both parties simply work together to draw districts that often protect incumbents.

Why does redistricting matter?

Redistricting affects political power. It determines which party controls Congress, state, and local governments across the country. Even when the population is divided equally, drawing the lines one way can reward Democrats and punish Republicans or vice versa. Some line drawing can protect incumbents. Some line drawing can guarantee they will face a potent challenger, either from their own party or the opposite party. Consequently, redistricting has a direct bearing on which matters a legislature chooses to tackle and which to ignore.

Solutions include the following:

- Mail in election ballots as done in the state of Oregon.
- Allow an independent commission to oversee redistricting as done in Nevada.

- After a convicted felon has served their time, allow them the opportunity to fully integrate back into society by allowing them the opportunity to vote.
- As occurred in the 2018 midterm elections, if you hold an office or position that oversees state election, then you should give up that oversight authority if you decide to run for statewide office.
- No changes to voter registration and polling should be permitted within six months of any election. Any entity who may oppose such changes should be given ample opportunity to legally challenge such changes prior to any election date.

Admissions/Qualifications at Institutions of Higher Learning

The Civil Rights Act of 1964 made it illegal to discriminate against students and college applicants on the basis of race or gender, but proving bias in college admissions is quite difficult. As with discrimination in the hiring process, rejected applicants generally are not privy to the factors behind the decisions made by admissions personnel. As a result, many schools adopted so-called *affirmative action* policies to help ensure greater diversity. Methods vary, but affirmative action refers to the special consideration given to women, racial minorities, and members of other historically excluded groups.

Just because federal courts have backed affirmative action in college admissions doesn't mean the practice has been embraced by the states. In fact, the Supreme Court in 2014 upheld Michigan's constitutional amendment banning affirmative action in the state's universities. So while federal law currently permits such policies, they may be further defined—or even eliminated—through state laws.

At least ten states have passed laws limiting or banning the use of affirmative action in college admissions, including the following:

- Oklahoma: State question 759, passed by voter referendum in 2012, prohibits the state from granting preferential treatment to certain individuals, including that based on race, in public education.
- Arizona: Proposition 107, passed by ballot initiative in 2010, prohibits the granting of preferential treatment of certain individuals, including that based on race, in public education.

- Nebraska: Initiative 424, passed by voters in 2008, eliminates affirmative action at state colleges and universities.
- Texas: The 10 percent plan, passed by lawmakers in 1997, guarantees state university and college admission of students who finish in the top 10 percent of their graduating class, thus narrowing the application of affirmative action policies.
- Florida: The One Florida initiative, issued as an executive order by Governor Jeb Bush in 1999, prohibits the use of affirmative action for the admissions policies of state schools.

Health Care/Medical Insurance

The US ranks dead last in life expectancy for men and second to last for women among the seventeen wealthiest nations. Infant mortality in the US ranks last among the most advanced countries in the world. And worse, among the thirty-four most developed countries, US health care outcomes fell from twentieth to twenty-seventh from 1990 to 2010.

The world's richest economy scores dismally no matter which health care measures we examine.

Why so bad?

One reason the US ranks so poorly globally is that health outcomes for certain racial, ethnic, and socioeconomic groups fare so poorly domestically. African Americans, Latinos, and the economically disadvantaged experience poorer health care access and lower quality of care than White Americans. And in most measures, that gap is growing.

"Your health care depends on who you are," according to a 2014 report from the Robert Wood Johnson Foundation, the nation's largest philanthropy dedicated to health. "Race and ethnicity continue to influence a patient's chances of receiving many specific health care interventions and treatments."

The foundation estimates Latinos and African Americans experience 30 to 40 percent poorer health outcomes than White Americans. This disparity leads not only to shortened lives and increased illness but also costs the nation more than $60 billion in lost productivity each year.

Media/Social Media/Technology/Entertainment Industry Impact

With respect to major media outlets, name one major media outlet other than Black Entertainment Television (BET) and the Weather Channel that is owned by an African American. In 2013, minorities owned just 6 percent of commercial television stations in the country, 6 percent of FM radio stations, and 11 percent of AM radio stations.

With a few notable exceptions—the cable network BET launched in 1980 and TV One followed in 1995—African American ownership remains particularly low, hovering at less than 1 percent of all television properties and less than 2 percent of radio. Last year in fact, just two television stations were owned by black owners. That number is up to about ten today.

The argument here is simple: the news slant or direction can generally be expected to be tilted toward the views of the owner and shareholders. As an owner, I would cater to my viewership, and if my viewership is predominately one way, it's only good business to accommodate whoever the majority of my viewership is. I am not advocating that this approach is wrong. I am advocating, however, that this revelation is very real. As a result, if African Americans do not own a major media outlet or are not the targeted primary viewership, then it would be smart to evaluate the quality of output being distributed.

Other: Hate groups in the US remain on the rise, according to a new study.

The Southern Poverty Law Center identified 954 groups as hate groups, which it defines as "an organization that—based on its official statements or principles, the statements of its leaders, or its activities—has beliefs or practices that attack or malign an entire class of people, typically for their immutable characteristics." That number was up from 917 in 2016 and 892 in 2015.

Much of the rise took place inside the white supremacist movement. The number of neo-Nazi groups grew from ninety-nine to 121, anti-Muslim groups grew from 101 to 114, and anti-immigrant groups grew from fourteen to twenty-two. The law center asserted that the growth among white supremacists was fueled in large part by racially divisive language and actions by some present-day politicians.

Heidi Beirich, director of the Southern Poverty Law Center Intelligence Project, stated, "2018 has been a year that has seen increasing divisiveness and bigotry, particularly in mainstream American life." There has been a substantial emboldening of the radical right, and that is largely due to the actions of many within the current administration.

The report designates hate groups as anti-lesbian, gay, bisexual, and transgender (LGBT) organizations; antigovernment militias; and black nationalist groups, including the Nation of Islam, which professes anti-Semitic, anti-white, and anti-LGBT rhetoric. It points out that those groups should not be confused with "mainstream black activist groups such as Black Lives Matter that work to eliminate systemic racism in American society and its institutions."

Perhaps surprisingly, the number of Ku Klux Klan groups dropped dramatically from 130 to seventy-two, an indication, the law center says, that the 150-year-old organization has little appeal for a new generation of white supremacists.

Hate Crimes Update As of November 2018

According to the *New York Times*, of the more than 7,100 hate crimes reported in 2017, nearly three out of five were motivated by race and ethnicity. Religion and sexual orientation were the other two primary motivators.

But hate crimes remain vastly underreported. Only 12.6 percent of the agencies in the Federal Bureau of Investigations (FBI) report indicated that hate crimes had occurred in their jurisdictions in 2017. Data shows that hate crime victims often do not trust that reporting will help them.

The FBI said it planned to train law enforcement officers next year on how to do a better job of identifying and reporting bias-motivated incidents. The justice department has also launched a new website on hate crimes. "The Department of Justice's top priority is to reduce violent crime in America, and hate crimes are violent crimes. They are also despicable violations of our core values as Americans." This was cited in a November 13, 2018 *New York Times* article by John Eligon, Hate Crimes Increase for the third Consecutive Year, F.B.I. Reports.

The offenses in hate crimes vary in severity from murder to vandalism. Black people accounted for nearly half of hate crime victims last year, according to the FBI report. Of those targeted based on religion, 58 percent were Jewish.

Much of the country's political discourse in recent years has been fueled by deep racial divisions. According to the NAACP, the organization began to see an increase during the presidential elections in 2015. As noted by the NAACP, "The level of tribalism that was being fueled by presidential candidates, the acceptance of intolerance that has been condoned by politicians and many others across the country has simply emboldened individuals to be more open and notorious with their racial hatred."

How was I shaped and motivated by chapter eight?
Simply, I am shaped and motivated by my experiences. As far back as I can remember, race and racism have remained front and center throughout my life. When you have spent a lifetime on the receiving end, you develop an *instinctive antenna* that instantly emits an alert when something does not feel or look right. Based on the current climate, it appears that these issues are not going away any time soon.

The current-day battlefield is not about us; it is about future generations. It's about the seed that you plant today and the harvest it will yield tomorrow. Considering all that is at stake, ignorance, apathy, and complacency are no longer acceptable excuses.

Awareness and a willingness to do something are the cornerstones to establishing a path to possible solutions. The battlefield involving race and racism probably will never cease to exist. Simply, the weaponry—methods of delivery—have changed, but the day-to-day tactics remain unchanged. Chapter eight, The Modern-Day Battlefield, is my recognition of this modern-day reality.

The minute we look away, the minute we stop fighting back, that's the minute bigotry wins.

—DaShanne Stokes

CHAPTER 9

Building a Legacy, Mentoring, and Role Modeling

We are reminded that, in the fleeting time we have on this earth, what matters is not wealth, or status, or power, or fame, but rather how well we have loved and what small part we have played in making the lives of others better.
—Barack Obama

THOUGHTS OF BUILDING A LEGACY, mentoring, and role modeling start at home. Hatred, right versus wrong, ethics, respect, moral standards, and integrity are either taught or modeled in the home environment as well.

My daughters were fascinated to hear the stories told in and outside the confines of this publication; though somewhat painful, this pleased me. I have come to realize that it does not matter what side of the equation you sit on; knowledge and truth will liberate you. I also realized I had a duty, a responsibility, and an obligation to others, my daughters, and myself to reveal truth. Also, at this stage of my life, I am seeking a higher fulfillment that is much larger than me. That higher fulfillment involves:

- Giving back
- Helping and informing others
- Community engagement
- Mentoring
- Role modeling
- Legacy building

Why is it so important to know and understand your ancestral family history/tree?

- Discovering family history can become a teachable moment for kids
- Reconnecting with long-lost family or extended family
- Preserving the legacy of a beloved relative
- Preserving family traditions
- Researching how ancestors were involved in history
- Updating facts and concerns about family medical history

Two of the most important race-sensitive events in my lifetime were the assassination of the Reverend Dr. Martin Luther King Jr. and the election of President Barrack Obama. Why? What did these two events mean?

I was eleven years old when Dr. Martin Luther King Jr. was killed. I knew his death was significant because of the emotional reaction from my mother. Outside of church or religious-connected activities, I seldom if ever recall seeing her cry or become overly emotional. Later on, as I studied history and began to understand the plight of people of color, I began to truly understand the iconic status of the Reverend Dr. Martin Luther King Jr. A unifier. A man who appealed to the social consciousness of all men. Bravery. Leadership personified. Purpose-driven. Educated. Articulate. Confident. Great orator. Powerful. These are the same personal attributes that put fear into the hearts of those who had opposing points of view. Ironically today, those who have opposing points of view are still fearful of these same personal attributes.

In my mind, the election of Barack Obama revealed two basic achievements and/or extremes. One, the country was led to believe that the US had overcome a major hurdle and achieved a major milestone by electing its first president of color. I use the phrase "of color" because President Obama's mother was Caucasian and from the Midwest while his father was from Nigeria. I am reminded of that silly, made-up rule that if one parent is black, then the offspring is automatically black—not multicultural but black. Quite honestly, I never thought I'd see a black president during my lifetime. I was also grateful that so many elderly African Americans were able to witness this historic event before they reached the end of their natural lives.

The presidency of Barack Obama brought hope to those without hope. For many who had doubted democracy, their doubt was temporarily restored. Secondly, after an approximate forty-year *Crock-Pot* rate of progress, the post presidency of President Obama created an atmosphere that reminded us of what the raw, underbelly of racism really looked like. It's as if people of color said to themselves, "We knew all along that deep within the hearts of man, nothing really had changed." In fact, there is little trust and a lack of confidence that politicians on the national level have the best interest of all people in mind. Many would argue that lobbyists, major corporations, and big donors have hijacked our national political process.

I love talking to mature and respected elders who possess wisdom about topics of historical significance. Their oral accounts of history fascinate me. I advocate that we simply cannot afford to lose the civil rights aspect of our history. An old biblical proverb reveals, "What has been will be again, what has been done will be done again; there is nothing new under the sun." Our connection between what was and what will be is through the eyes and wisdom of those who have already traveled the path(s) we are embarking on today.

Mentors and elders within the family unit can be viewed as our modern-day connection to imparting wisdom and establishing all-important legacies. Why do we need these people in our lives? Generally, they:

1. Provide information and knowledge
2. Can help us improve and overcome
3. Find ways to stimulate our personal and professional growth
4. Offer free counsel, which makes them priceless in more ways than one
5. Are disciplinarians creating necessary boundaries that we cannot set for ourselves

6. Offer insightfulness
7. Can be connectors to the past, present, and future
8. Have the experiences you can learn from

There have been several men and women in my life who helped shape me, impacted me in a mighty way. For this project, I want to focus on the men. Impactful men were rare during my early, formative years. For the most part, engagement with impactful men originated from outside of the traditional family unit. You see, except in one instance, my immediate, traditional family unit was void of male role models. In many of my mentor-coach relationships, the teacher or mentor was never formally asked to be a mentor. These relationships evolved and flourished through a genuine likeness and admiration for each other. Several of these men I admired from a distance. While their names may remain meaningless to you, it is appropriate to identify some of them as I share the impact they had on me. You see, it's not about who they were; it's about what they shared. It's about the spirit they possessed, it's about the patience they displayed, and it's about the genuine care they had for others.

Mr. Smith, from the Neighborhood

A senior citizen with limited education. Always had a smile on his face. Fast talker. Even though we were living in a small, rural town in the Panhandle, the late Mr. Smith had spent a considerable amount of time living in Miami. As I reflect, this little tidbit is probably what made Mr. Smith all the more interesting. The neighborhood checkers legend. For those who may not know, checkers is a game played on a checkered board (small, painted piece of plywood) with tops from pop bottles as maneuverable pieces. He was the best I've ever encountered at talking *smack* in the midst of competition. Each time we played, I had zero chance of defeating him. Usually, a game between skilled opponents often exceeded ten minutes; it was not unusual for our games to be over within two minutes or less. This man was easily thirty years my senior, but he made time for me.

What could this man possibly teach me? He taught me that even though you may be a master at your craft, always take the time to help develop others. He also taught me to not be afraid to confront what may appear to be insurmountable odds. He taught me to think, act, and talk *on my feet*. I am thoroughly convinced that my one-on-one time with Mr. Smith helped me once I started playing organized sports, and it also helped me later in business when I was forced to think quickly on my feet. Since I cannot recall ever beating Mr. Smith, this requires me to dig deep to withdraw something positive about the constant whippings I received. The point here is oftentimes just getting in the game can offer tremendous opportunities and insight. Those opportunities and insight include developing hard and soft life skills, dealing with adversity, and overcoming what appear to be insurmountable odds.

Robert, a.k.a. R. B.

R. B. was my late brother-in-law. He was the first black man and family member I had the opportunity to observe up close and personal as a husband, live-in father, and provider. He had no children of his own, but he raised two children who were not his biological offspring. R. B. was active in practicing his faith. He was deeply involved in the community. As an example of his community involvement, he would coach and provide transportation for a community-assembled baseball team. Outside of his regular work, R. B. would also perform little side jobs for others where they would compensate him for his work. His primary source of income was working as a veterinarian assistant. As I grew older, R. B. and I would have some of the most eye-opening conversations I'd ever had about life, challenges, and racism. I also thought he was the coolest. R. B. was my very first husband role model. As he grew older, he spent a lot of quiet time just sitting and reflecting; I now see the value in just sitting, meditating, and reflecting. I don't recall ever hearing him raise his voice out of anger. He was gentle and caring. In my view, he had a PhD in dealing with people.

Staff Sergeant (S.Sgt.) Stolze, First Military Supervisor

I first encountered the now deceased S.Sgt. Stolze when I deployed to Germany after completing army basic training and advanced individual training. S.Sgt. Stolze could fool you by his appearance. He was rotund and rather gruff looking with a very serious demeanor and raspy voice. He was not an educated man. Rumor or legend revealed he had been reduced in rank on more than one occasion. S.Sgt. Stolze taught me how to take advantage of professional opportunities.

He was the master at attention to detail. He taught me how to be the best you can be. He taught and instilled excellence in his crew. S.Sgt. Stolze emphasized the importance of training, not just training as we know it but training the right way with purpose and intent. He emphasized repetition until his standards were met. The color of a man's skin did not matter to him. Over time and as I became a supervisor and manager, I tried to instill in others what this man had instilled in me. Under his supervision I won numerous, prestigious individual and corporate awards and recognitions. Everyone who worked for him was widely called a super trooper. He created an environment where the internal competition among his team was more intense than the external competition. Professionally, he had more of an impact on me than any other single person.

Mr. Shepherd, Mentor

He was twenty years my senior. An entrepreneur, small business owner, and veteran. He was the first entrepreneur of color who I developed a personal relationship with. Shepherd had a very nice home in an upscale community with a picturesque background of Mt. Rainier in Washington State. He was full of wisdom. Shepherd taught me and showed me that I could gain exposure to things I never dreamed of. He exposed me to the finer things in life. He taught me the value of business relationships. One of my greatest regrets was when I left the Pacific Northwest, where he lived; I thought of him often but failed to maintain contact. After about five years had passed, I attempted to locate him up and discovered he had passed away. After this experience, I vowed that I would never again allow myself to lose contact with people that I deeply care about.

Mr. Hubbard, Mentor

He was thirty years my senior. Retired military man, elder, deacon, family man, mentor, accountability partner, well respected by many, and a confidant. He went on to a successful second career after his military retirement. Truly, in my eyes, this man was an older version of what I'd hoped to become. He set the example for family and faith, full of wisdom. Mr. Hubbard exposed me to the importance of living a holistic lifestyle. He encouraged me to grow in my faith. He taught me the importance of servant leadership. Eddie Hubbard taught me humbleness and how to lead by a firm, quiet example. I had the awesome honor of speaking at his funeral as a dear friend.

What did I learn from these experiences?

There is direct, and then there's indirect mentorship. I came to realize that you may make an impact in the lives of others, even during encounters and situations where you may not realize you are making an impact. Even when known, I did not ask anyone for a mentorship/coach/ accountability partner relationship. In most cases, our like-minded spirits and our genuine fondness for one another brought us together. You felt it. You knew there was a connection, and as a result of this connection, relationships manifested themselves into something meaningful. We all need our personal executive advisory board in the form of mentors. I advocate having a mentor is a step in the right direction; however, to be the best you can be requires a multitude of counselors.

Once others begin to view me as a mentor, I would often tell younger men that the most valuable giveaway I could share with them was my time. You cannot recapture time; I had to see some potential in you before I invested my time.

Each of these men were older, full of wisdom, patient, and possessed a willingness to help others.

The meaning of life is to find your gift. The purpose of life is to give it away.
—Pablo Picasso

Find and Become a Mentor

How do you choose a mentor? What are the criteria for selecting a mentor? In choosing, there is no right way or wrong way. Depending on you and who you're going to ask, the approach can be subtle or bold. Sometimes the mentor and mentee find each other. Over time, I've just focused on developing a relationship with a person, and eventually the relationship developed into a mentoring relationship. Here are some of the qualities that you should look for in a mentor:

- Maturity
- Experience
- Accomplishment

- Earned respect
- Integrity
- Good reputation
- Availability
- An example to others

This is not an all-inclusive list; it is an essential start that can be modified.

There is a distinct difference between professional mentoring and personal mentoring. It is not unusual to have multiple mentors. Different mentors bring different levels of knowledge and subject matter expertise to the table.

I have been fortunate to live, work, and vacation in several places within the continental United States and abroad. As I was writing this book, I pondered how my foreign travel experiences would fit within the context of what I was trying to convey in *It's As Plain As Black and White: How Race and Racism Shaped and Motivated Me*. I concluded there is some relevance.

Let me start by saying a large percentage of my domestic and foreign traveling experiences have been positive as it relates to race and racism. During my travels, I have tried to be a positive representative of myself, my culture, and my country. With this approach, people have generally reacted positively toward me, particularly in situations where my family and I were the only ones of color in our surroundings at the time. I believe that if you carry yourself in a respectful manner, you will be treated with respect. In many instances, I have felt somewhat empowered. This empowerment was the result of others valuing my intellect more than the color of my skin. There have been situations where I felt more at ease abroad than I did in certain places on American soil. Even with its shortcomings, I believe there is still no place like the United States of America.

At the end of the day, I am imploring you to be a good ambassador. Ambassadorship may not be embraced by many. One of the reasons for rejecting the idea of ambassadorship may include a lack of understanding of how your actions can negatively or positively reflect on others. Other reasons may include a lack of self-confidence, self-worth, or exposure to environments beyond our own. As part of something greater than ourselves, our actions and reactions toward how we deal with racism and injustice are bigger than any one individual. Don't identify with stereotypes—identify with your individual uniqueness.

Know and recognize that others may be judged, elevated, or denied based on your actions, conduct, and behavior. If you fail to see the value in ambassadorship, then there probably isn't anything I can say to you that would change your way of thinking.

We all should be campaigners, representatives, promoters, champions, supporters, backers, and boosters for whoever we are and whatever we represent.

Sensitivity toward others or recognizing the elephant in the room is a declining art form. Inclusiveness and making others feel comfortable in certain settings are no longer priorities. Civility is largely ignored. The big fish are only interested in swallowing up the little fish. There is a not-so-subtle power grab. For many, it's as if we live in a state of anarchy. This is our new norm.

> *No man is an island, entire of itself; every man is a piece of the continent, a part of the main.*
>
> —John Donne

How was I shaped and motivated by chapter nine?

No man is an island. Our families, friends, associates, and society as a whole, everyone is impacted by race and racism. It does not matter what side of the aisle you reside on, as a nation, as a people, and as a family we are only as strong as our weakest link. All of us have a vested interest in this reality.

We stand on the shoulders of others who came before us. We owe a great debt of gratitude to the sacrifices, commitment, and the dedication of others. The best way for us to honor our trailblazers and elders is to share with others what positive and life-changing lessons we learned. Our lives should be a continuation of their legacies.

With regard to giving back, many of us may think we may not have much to give, but we can willingly give what we have! This is not a cliché; we are all truly blessed to be a blessing to others. We are truly blessed to be in the unique position of dedicating ourselves to developing, mentoring, and setting an example for others. I am a product of the famous African proverb that reminds us, "It takes a village to raise a child." Without the help of others, I cannot begin to comprehend how different my journey would have been. I believe each of us were created to make this world a better place, one person at a time.

We can achieve this goal by simply passing to others what we have learned. For me, chapter nine, Building a Legacy, Mentoring, and Role Modeling, is a step in the direction toward attempting to positively impact the lives of others.

> *For to be free is not merely to cast off one's chains, but to live in a way that respects and enhances the freedom of others.*
>
> —Nelson Mandela

CHAPTER 10

What Role Does the Church and Faith Play in Addressing Racism, Bias, and Injustice?

But the church as a whole has been all too negligent on the question of civil rights. It has too often blessed a status quo that needed to be blasted, and reassured a social order that needed to be reformed.
—Martin Luther King Jr.

Injustice?

IN THIS FINAL CHAPTER, I am presenting a perspective that, in my opinion, is widely discussed among a diverse cross section of people who practice faith in their everyday lives. What role does the church and faith play in addressing racism, bias, and injustice? Chapter ten is written in a mostly rhetorical narrative. Concrete solutions to complex issues are complicated. As a result of the complicated nature of racism, bias, and injustice, this final chapter is written to encourage inner perspective, reflection, and thought rather than find solutions.

Have you ever wondered why a sovereign God would allow bias and injustice to occur among mankind? Have you ever wondered why a sovereign God would allow a people to endure unwarranted suffering at the hands of another people who are perceived to be in power in government, politics, and the economy? This is similar to people questioning why natural disasters and calamities are allowed to occur. I do not know the mind of Christ, but I do believe that God is ultimately in control of everything he created. Ultimately, there is a divine master plan that is beyond man's comprehension. In due time, God's plan will be revealed.

With that being said, I am deeply troubled about how those among us who are faith practitioners are able to tolerate or turn a blind eye to racial bias, prejudice, wrongdoing, and injustice. If people of faith rush to help others who may experience a natural disaster or calamity, why wouldn't they do the same for someone who may be experiencing institutionalized and prolonged injustice and bias? The Bible speaks of a double-minded man. A double-minded man is a person drawn in two opposite directions. His allegiance is divided and because of his lack of sincerity, he vacillates between belief and disbelief. Truth is truth and is unwavering. Could it be that we are just selective about who and what issues we decide to support? Could it be that we view these type of issues from our own perspective rather than from the perspective of our true faith? Could it be that because of our human frailties, we simply cannot fully comprehend what would Jesus do if he was faced with our current-day dilemmas?

Have you ever wondered how people of faith can openly claim their belief yet privately and sometimes publicly struggle with denouncing bias and racism? The written word is specific and clear, yet there is a problem among people of faith. Is the problem related to interpretation, selective adherence to what is written and taught, or selfish ambitions? Could it be we are simply human, an imperfect creation created by a perfect creator? Could it be that we are simply too weak and too flawed that we cannot achieve what the creator intended for us to achieve? This is not a white problem, and this is not a black problem; this is a human problem. If you regularly attend church, how often have you heard a pastor examine the topics of race and racism within the church and among its members? If your answer is seldom, then the follow-up question is why? Are these topics too controversial? Will the congregation experience conviction and be made to feel too uncomfortable? Is there a perceived threat of possible congregational backlash toward the messenger?

What is the role of the modern-day church with respect to injustice and inequality? If you are a person of faith, shouldn't the ill treatment of any human being trouble you? Is there a universal message from the church about bias and injustice? Or does the church have a universal problem with interpretation and application of what is revealed in the written word? Something is amiss within the church and among believers. What is it? Not just African American churches, but what role if any should all churches engage in today, as it relates to overcoming social injustice and inequality? The concept of universal love among people of faith should not be one that is too complex to understand. Should churches do more? Are the dynamics between what the church should be supporting versus what makes its parishioners comfortable so vastly different?

First, let's examine the role of the church from a historical perspective. During the height of the civil rights movement, African American Christians saw the church as a familiar and safe place to be during the chaotic civil rights movement. Many who were impacted went there daily to pray for liberation or to meet with their neighbors and friends in a comfortable environment. A common opinion was that oppression, rejection, and segregation leave a human being with no one to turn to but God. The deep-rooted love of religion goes back to the days of slavery as African American ancestors looked to God for freedom just as they are doing today. Perhaps the importance of the church is what drove those who were in favor of segregation to attack, bomb, and burn black churches across the South. Regardless of the uneasiness felt by African American Christians, the church remained a pillar of hope and stability. During the civil rights movement, nearly every African American community had at least one church that provided tangible, moral, and spiritual support. Mass meetings and rallies in support of the movement were held at large African American churches. Offerings of money were taken up to provide financial support to those participating in civil rights activities, for instance by helping jailed demonstrators to make bail and pay various other fines. These actions by African American Christians strengthened the bond not only to one another but to God as well. Following the civil rights movement, dozens of influential churches in Alabama, Georgia, Tennessee, and Oklahoma were designated as historic landmarks.

For those of us who lived through the movement decades ago, especially those of us who are African Americans, we can attest to the huge role the church played during a time full of hatred and violence. According to research, there have been at least one hundred attacks on black churches since 1956. More than thirty black churches were burned in an eighteen-month period in 1995–1996. This led Congress to pass the Church Arson Prevention Act of 1996.

The church proved steadfast in ending segregation and providing African Americans the rights all American citizens deserved. Regardless of one's beliefs, it is clear that the church provided hope and inspiration to those fighting for liberty in a time when the words "hope" and "inspiration" were scarcely used.

As I was celebrating a recent Martin Luther King Jr. Day in the quiet of my own home, I realized there is another small role the church can play in promoting racial equality. Not all churches honor the legacy of Dr. King on this national holiday. Is it possible that even some predominately African American churches fail to mention or honor this day? For many, of different ethnic backgrounds, the church may be the only opportunity where public acknowledgment of the significance of Dr. King's contributions are even heard. This idea is bolstered by the fact that Dr. King was an established theologian representing the betterment for all. In my opinion, the church should be a model of unity for all of society.

One of Martin Luther King's most famous quotes concerns racial segregation and the American church. "It is appalling that the most segregated hour of Christian America is eleven o'clock on Sunday morning," King remarked in 1963.

Sadly, more than fifty years later, the church remains overwhelmingly racially divided. Only between 5 and 7.5 percent of churches in the US are considered to be racially diverse, a designation meaning that at least 20 percent of a church's members don't belong to the predominant racial group there.

"Ninety percent of African American Christians worship in all-black churches. Ninety percent of White American Christians worship in all-white churches," noted Chris Rice, coauthor of *More Than Equals: Racial Healing for the Sake of the Gospel*. "Years since the incredible victories of the civil rights movement, we continue to live in the trajectory of racial fragmentation. The biggest problem is that we don't see that as a problem."

I am a member of a predominately African American church. Whenever we have guests visit us who are of another race, if I am near them, I go out of my way to try to make them feel welcome. There is something within me that compels me to reach out. I have been in situations where the roles were reversed, and I can honestly say, when others reached out to me in these situations, it comforted my spirit.

Human value cannot be equated with race, wealth, social standing, or educational level. All are significant and valuable in God's eyes. To regard a race, group, or individual as less important than another is uncharacteristically troubling in view of the fact that Christ died for all people. At the foot of the cross, we are all equal, both in our worth to God—he sent his son to die for each of us—and our need to accept His gift of salvation. We must learn to respect and honor every person regardless of their place or color. Christ said, "Truly I tell you, whatever you did not do for one of the least of these, you did not do for me" (Matthew 25:45 NIV).

As I search the written word, there is a common theme relating to race and racism. You do not have to be a religious scholar or pastor to comprehend what is revealed in various scripture. That common theme includes the following common words or statements:

- One body
- Do not judge
- Love one another
- Love your neighbor
- Show compassion
- Show no partiality
- Unity

Humankind is a universal family. We live in a single world community. No race or nation has the right to look down on or disassociate itself from another. Christianity supports there are only two divisions of humankind—the saved and the unsaved. Other differences are merely skin deep or culturally flavored, but all people are relatives. Social concerns cannot biblically be divorced from the walk of faith. The principles by which man will be judged are their treatment of those who are hungry, homeless, poor, diseased, and imprisoned.

It would be excusable for me or anyone else who has experienced racial disparities to hate. To hate is a very strong personal reaction toward any human being. A group or individual who has committed wrongdoing is not a reason to hate. I know so many people who have had similar experiences like my experiences who also share my view on hate or not to hate. I am so thankful that a spiritual balance was instilled in me that no matter how others may treat me or no matter what was done to me, hate is not and was not a proper response under any set of circumstances.

What does the Bible say about racism?

The first thing to understand in this discussion is that there is only one race—the human race. Caucasians, Africans, Asians, Indians, Arabs, and Jews are not different races. Rather, they are different ethnicities of the human race. All human beings have the same physical characteristics, with minor variations of course. More importantly, all human beings are equally created in the image and likeness of God (Genesis 1:26–27 NIV).

God does not show partiality or favoritism, and neither should we. James 2:4 describes those who discriminate as "judges with evil thoughts." Instead, we are to love our neighbors as ourselves. In the Old Testament, God divided humanity into two *racial* groups: Jews and Gentiles. God's intent was for the Jews to be a kingdom of priests, ministering to the Gentile nations. Instead, for the most part, the Jews became proud of their status and despised the Gentiles. Jesus Christ put an end to this, destroying the dividing wall of hostility. All forms of racism, prejudice, and discrimination are affronts to the work of Christ on the cross.

Jesus commands us to love one another as He loves us. If God is impartial and loves us with impartiality, then we need to love others with that same high standard. Jesus teaches in Matthew 25 that whatever we do to the least of His brothers, we do to Him. If we treat a person with contempt, we are mistreating a person created in God's image; we are hurting somebody whom God loves and for whom Jesus died.

Roughly seven in ten (72 percent) Americans say they believe in heaven. Heaven is defined as the place of everlasting blessedness of the righteous, the abode of departed spirits. The eternal kingdom. Without going too deep, if you are a Christian and Bible believer and you practice racism and bigotry, life in the hereafter is not color conscious or segregated. We will all have to confront our inadequacies one day.

I have addressed the issues of racism, bias, and injustice among believers from a corporate perspective. The question remains, as individuals, if you are believers of the faith, what can you do to end racism, bias, and injustice?

On Sunday, October 7, 2018, my pastor preached a sermon titled, "What are you doing with what you've been through?" I thought the message was very real and relevant to my approach of taking a negative situation like race and racism and turning it into a positive. The following key points were lifted from his message:

- Learn to embrace the positive and negative experiences in your life.
- God doesn't hurt people!
- Experience is schooling, so make certain you extract the lesson.
- The experience you go through should equip you to be a model, a motivational speaker, and a qualified minister.
- The experience that you resent the most will often be your greatest ministry.
- If you don't share your painful experiences, the only thing that will come out of them is pain.

Any religion that professes to be concerned about the souls of men and is not concerned about the slums that damn them, the economic conditions that strangle them, and the social conditions that cripple them is a spiritually moribund religion awaiting burial.

—Reverend Dr. Martin Luther King Jr.

How was I shaped and motivated by chapter ten?

I was exposed to church and faith-based values very early in life. As a result of this exposure, I learned to view and handle adversity in ways that are aligned with my faith-based upbringing.

Human value cannot be equated with race, wealth, social standing, or educational level. All are significant and valuable in God's eyes. We must learn to respect and honor every person and all people regardless of their circumstances or color. Humankind is a universal family. No race or nation has the right to look down on or disassociate itself from another.

History reflects the church played a major role in the African American civil rights movement by providing financial, spiritual, safety, legal, and physical comfort to those in need. In my view, the modern-day church should continue to reject inequality and injustice by reinforcing and encouraging consistent truth, honesty, and change in the hearts of men.

Can individuals do more to curb racism, bias, and injustice? Should the church become an advocate for the disadvantaged? Yes, individuals and the church can and should do more. Do those who practice their faith have an obligation and responsibility to be a shining example for the rest of the world? Again, I believe the answer is yes. I believe the church's role is to judge the church. It's the creator's role to judge the world. If the church would simply do its part, those of us in the church would be leading advocates against bias and injustice whenever and wherever it occurs.

Prior to retirement, my position was often a catalyst for high stress. As a result of this tension, periodically I would take the short drive down to the Gulf to spend some quiet, alone time to destress. The sounds and scenery associated with the coastline can be very relaxing. At the locations I chose, you could drive your vehicle right up to the water's edge. This was an area that did not have a high-density African American population. On one particular occasion, I was alone on a stretch of beach, meditating and reflecting, minding my own business. As I looked along the horizon of the shoreline, I saw an older model car speeding toward me. This was midday on a weekday; there were no other beachgoers in sight. As the car got closer, I noticed a young female occupant with her head and upper body hanging out of the backseat window. Her hair was flying in the wind. I braced myself for some type of unwelcomed harassment. As the car got parallel to me, what happened next totally stunned me. As the car sped by, the young female yelled at me, "God bless you, sir!" I was left speechless. It's moments like this that give me hope.

Since my faith and the church played a prominent role in my upbringing, it would only be conceivable for me to be influenced, shaped, and motivated by my faith-based values. This influenced me to close out this project with chapter ten, What Role Does the Church and Faith Play in Addressing Racism, Bias, and Injustice?

That's a Wrap

At some point during my upbringing, I developed a humanitarian attitude and an interest in a world view, advocating humanity for all. I can recall an assignment in an African American literature class when the instructor asked each member of the class to name three things we would like to experience in the world. My response was: (1) respect for all mankind, (2) a world without hunger, and (3) a world with peace and prosperity for all. I'm not exactly sure when this attitude was given birth, but it was evident early in my life. This mind-set drove me in every phase of my life. Even though I was raised in a lower social-economic neighborhood, I dreamed of equality, justice, and a healthy respect toward everyone. I tried to model my life, emphasizing these attributes.

During research for this project, I sought advice from and interaction with a few friends that are a generation before me. I stumbled upon something that somewhat startled me, many of these elders felt it too painful to even discuss this project. They find discussions, movies, and documentaries about the past, race and racism too painful. This discovery revealed the true gravity and impact of how bigotry and hatred can affect the entire lives of so many who have been recipients of this social cancer.

I realize that I, alone, cannot solve racism! No one person can! Solving racism is not my goal. I want to inspire people. I want to help create an atmosphere where respectful, open and honest dialogue is encouraged. I want to be a conduit for hope, illustrating that despite disadvantages, success is always possible.

As a country and as a people, we have made great strides toward racial equality during my lifetime. Fast-forward to today, many of those great strides have either been diminished or marginalized. It appears that today, division, politics, and an unwillingness to compromise and express empathy for others is the new standard. If true, we live in perilous times, but there is always hope.

As I engage others, many agree that generally there is a moral decline in society. So what exactly can we do? Do we circle the wagons and only focus on ourselves and our own self-interest? Do we seek truth and honesty? What values do we espouse? What has happened to leadership? What role, if any, does the church play to address racial equality? Considering the divisiveness we encounter today, what do we say to our children? What world will our children inherit from us?

If this is my story in the twenty-first century, I cannot even begin to imagine the stories of those who preceded me. I have heard and read about them and how difficult their path was to racial equality and justice. I have even witnessed many of the things that I have heard and read about. But hearing and reading cannot replace what you witness and experience. When you experience such encounters, the effect on you can be a life changer, to say the least.

I refused to compromise my values, beliefs, and integrity. Even though others may appear to cross this ethical line of ignoring unfairness, bias, and bigotry with relative ease, I simply could not do it. The few times I was pushed during my career, I struggled with myself. At the end of the day, while I may have been forced to toe that proverbial ethical line, I thank God Almighty that I survived. I endured.

"A man who stands for nothing will fall for anything." This often-repeated quote by Malcolm X rings so true of our present-day situation.

APPENDIX 1

Constitutional Amendments and Major Civil Rights Acts of Congress

Amendment/ Act	Public Law/ US Code	Main Provisions
Thirteenth Amendment	PL 38–11; 13 Stat. 567; PL 38–52 13 Stat. 774–775	Abolished slavery and involuntary servitude, except as punishment for a crime; approved by the Thirty-Eighth Congress (1863–1865) as S.J. Res. 16; ratified by the states on December 6, 1865
Civil Rights Act of 1866	14 Stat. 27–30	Guaranteed the rights of all citizens to make and enforce contracts and to purchase, sell, or lease property; passed by the Thirty-Ninth Congress (1865–1867) as S.R. 61

Amendment/ Act	Public Law/ US Code	Main Provisions
Fourteenth Amendment	14 Stat. 358–359	Declared that all persons born or naturalized in the US were citizens and that any state that denied or abridged the voting rights of males over the age of twenty-one would be subject to proportional reductions in its representation in the US House of Representatives; approved by the Thirty-Ninth Congress (1865–1867) as H.J. Res. 127; ratified by the states on July 9, 1868
Fifteenth Amendment	P.L. 40–14; 15 Stat. 346	Forbade any state to deprive a citizen of his vote because of race, color, or previous condition of servitude; approved by the Fortieth Congress (1867–1869) as S.J. Res. 8; ratified by the states on February 3, 1870
First Ku Klux Klan Act (Civil Rights Act of 1870)	16 Stat. 140–146	Prohibited discrimination in voter registration on the basis of race, color, or previous condition of servitude; established penalties for interfering with a person's right to vote; gave federal courts the power to enforce the act and to employ the use of federal marshals and the army to uphold it; passed by the Forty-First Congress (1869–1871) as H.R. 1293

Amendment/ Act	Public Law/ US Code	Main Provisions
Second Ku Klux Klan Act (Civil Rights Act of 1871)	16 Stat. 433–440	Placed all elections in both the North and South under federal control; allowed for the appointment of election supervisors by federal circuit judges; authorized US marshals to employ deputies to maintain order at polling places; passed by the Forty-First Congress (1869–1871) as H.R. 2634
Third Ku Klux Klan Act (1871)	17 Stat. 13–15	Enforced the Fourteenth Amendment by guaranteeing all citizens of the United States the rights afforded by the Constitution and provided legal protection under the law; passed by the Forty-Second Congress (1871–1873) as H.R. 320
Civil Rights Act of 1875	18 Stat. 335–337	Barred discrimination in public accommodations and on public conveyances on land and water; prohibited exclusion of African Americans from jury duty; passed by the Forty-Third Congress (1873–1875) as H.R. 796

Amendment/ Act	Public Law/ US Code	Main Provisions
Civil Rights Act of 1957	P.L. 85–315; 71 Stat. 634	Created the six-member commission on civil rights and established the US Department of Justice Civil Rights Division; authorized the US Attorney General to seek court injunctions against deprivation and obstruction of voting rights by state officials; passed by the Eighty-Fifth Congress (1957–1959) as H.R. 6127
Civil Rights Act of 1960	P.L. 86–449; 74 Stat. 86	Expanded the enforcement powers of the Civil Rights Act of 1957 and introduced criminal penalties for obstructing the implementation of federal court orders; extended the US Commission on Civil Rights for two years; required that voting and registration records for federal elections be preserved; passed by the Eighty-Sixth Congress (1959–1961) as H.R. 8601

Amendment/ Act	Public Law/ US Code	Main Provisions
Civil Rights Act of 1964	P.L. 88–352; 78 Stat. 241	Prohibited discrimination in public accommodations, facilities, and schools; outlawed discrimination in federally funded projects; created the EEOC to monitor employment discrimination in public and private sectors; provided additional capacities to enforce voting rights; extended the US Commission on Civil Rights for four years; passed by the Eighty-Eighth Congress (1963–1965) as H.R. 7152
Voting Rights Act of 1965	P.L. 89–110; 79 Stat. 437	Suspended the use of literacy tests and voter disqualification devices for five years; authorized the use of federal examiners to supervise voter registration in states that used tests or in which less than half the voting-eligible residents registered or voted; directed the US Attorney General to institute proceedings against use of poll taxes; provided criminal penalties for individuals who violated the act; passed by the Eighty-Ninth Congress (1965–1967) as S. 1564

Amendment/ Act	Public Law/ US Code	Main Provisions
Civil Rights Act of 1968 (Fair Housing Act)	P.L. 90–284; 82 Stat. 73	Prohibited discrimination in the sale or rental of approximately 80 percent of the housing in the US; prohibited state governments and Native American tribal governments from violating the constitutional rights of Native Americans; passed by the Ninetieth Congress (1967–1969) as H.R. 2516
Voting Rights Act Amendments of 1970	P.L. 91–285; 84 Stat. 314	Extended the provisions of the Voting Rights Act of 1965 for five years; made the act applicable to areas where less than 50 percent of the eligible voting age population was registered as of November 1968; passed by the Ninety-First Congress (1969–1971) as H.R. 4249
Voting Rights Act Amendments of 1975	P.L. 94–73; 89 Stat. 400	Extended the provisions of the Voting Rights Act of 1965 for seven years; established coverage for other minority groups, including Native Americans, Hispanic Americans, and Asian Americans; permanently banned literacy tests; passed by the Ninety-Fourth Congress (1975–1977) as H.R. 6219

Amendment/ Act	Public Law/ US Code	Main Provisions
Voting Rights Act Amendments of 1982	P.L. 97–205; 96 Stat. 131	Extended for twenty-five years the provisions of the Voting Rights Act of 1965; allowed jurisdictions that could provide evidence of maintaining a clean voting rights record for at least ten years to avoid preclearance coverage (the requirement of federal approval of any change to local or state voting laws); provided for aid and instruction to disabled or illiterate voters; provided for bilingual election materials in jurisdictions with large minority populations; passed by the Ninety-Seventh Congress (1981–1983) as H.R. 3112
Civil Rights Restoration Act of 1987	P.L. 100–259; 102 Stat. 28	Established that antidiscrimination laws are applicable to an entire organization if any part of the organization receives federal funds; passed by the One-Hundredth Congress (1987–1989) as S. 557
Fair Housing Act Amendments of 1988	P.L. 100–430; 102 Stat. 1619	Strengthened the powers of enforcement granted to the Housing and Urban Development Department in the 1968 Fair Housing Act; passed by the One Hundredth Congress (1987–1989) as H.R. 1158

Amendment/ Act	Public Law/ US Code	Main Provisions
Civil Rights Act of 1991	P.L. 102–166; 105 Stat. 1071	Reversed nine US Supreme Court decisions (rendered between 1986 and 1991) that had raised the bar for workers who alleged job discrimination; provided for plaintiffs to receive monetary damages in cases of harassment or discrimination based on sex, religion, or disability; passed by the 102nd Congress (1991–1993) as S. 1745
Voting Rights Act of 2006	P.L. 109–246; 120 Stat. 577	Extended the provisions of the Voting Rights Act of 1965 for twenty-five years; extended the bilingual election requirements through August 5, 2032; directed the US Comptroller General to study and report to Congress on the implementation, effectiveness, and efficiency of bilingual voting materials requirements; passed by the 109th Congress (2005–2007) as H.R. 9

The Winding Road to Freedom—A Documentary Survey of Negro Experiences in America

—ᴀᴧ—

Jackson County Courthouse, a.k.a. The Plaza (date unknown)

Article Originally Published November 30, 1934

Jackson County is one of the four original counties of Florida. It has a population of approximately thirty thousand inhabitants of whom some two-thirds live on farms. Agriculture is the principal industry of the county. Cotton is the chief product, while tobacco, peanuts, lumbering and limestone products are produced in considerable quantities.

Prior to 1900, the Negro population greatly outnumbered the white but since that time it has steadily declined. It is estimated that between 40 and 45 percent of the population of Jackson County is at present Negro. Most of the old plantations have either been broken up or have been taken over by syndicates which work them now.

The county has the highest illiteracy rate of any in the state in proportion to the number of schools. There are no public libraries in the county. Negro teachers in the public schools receive from $25.00 to $35.00 per month. A recent survey of the county shows that between 75 and 80 percent of the citizens of Jackson County belong to either the Methodist or Baptist Church. Revivals are always eagerly and well attended.

Marianna, the county seat of Jackson County, has a population of about 3,300. The Negro populations between 35 and 40 percent. The town is on the main highway between Tallahassee and Mobile and is in line for considerable tourist trade.

It is a typical southern town with the general run of stores and a town square, except in Marianna the square is called, "the Plaza." The drug stores carry a large line of cheap detective, "wild west," and mystery magazines. *Time, The American Magazine, Cosmopolitan, Literary Digest, and Red Book* represent about the best available reading material to be purchased in the town.

The Winding Road to Freedom—Historical Wage Scale Excerpt

—w—

Chipola Hotel (date unknown)

Note: In 1934, this was the tallest building in Jackson County. Today, this building remains the tallest building in the county.

Article Originally Published November 30, 1934

In Jackson County, porters who worked in drug stores, grocery stores, etc., received from $4.00 to $6.00 per week. $2.25 per week is considered very good pay for domestic servants. $2.50 is considered extraordinarily well. Cooks in boarding houses during the tourist season receive around $3.00 per week. The bell boys in the Chipola Hotel receive $1.50 per week for twelve hours. Maids in the same hotel receive 44.00 per week for seven days work. Each maid has the care of an entire floor on nineteen rooms. The white waitresses in the dining room receive $4.00 per week plus tips. They work from 5:30 a.m. until 9 p.m. with time off between the main meals.

APPENDIX 4

National Advisory Commission on Civil Disorders—the Kerner Commission

—ⱍⱍⱍ—

The National Advisory Commission on Civil Disorders, known as the Kerner Commission after its chair, Governor Otto Kerner Jr. of Illinois, was an eleven-member presidential commission established by President Lyndon B. Johnson. The report was commissioned as Executive Order 11365 to investigate the causes of the 1967 race riots in the United States and to provide recommendations for the future.

> *Our nation is moving toward two societies—one black, one white—separate and unequal.*
>
> —Excerpt from the Kerner Report

The commission's charter was to explain the riots that plagued cities each summer since 1964 and to provide recommendations for the future. The commission's 1968 report, informally known as the Kerner Report, concluded that the nation was "moving toward two societies—one black, and one white—separate and un-equal." Unless conditions were remedied, the commission warned, the country faced a "system of apartheid" in its major cities. The Kerner Report delivered an indictment of *white society* for isolating and neglecting African Americans and urged legislation to promote racial integration and to enrich slums—primarily through the creation of jobs, job-training programs, and decent housing. President Johnson, however, rejected the recommendations. In April 1968, one month after the release of the Kerner Report, rioting broke out in more than one hundred cities following the assassination of civil rights leader Martin Luther King Jr. In the Kerner Report summary, the commission analyzed patterns in the riots and offered explanations for the disturbances. In 1998, thirty years after the issuance of the report, former senator and commission member Fred R. Harris coauthored a study that found the racial divide had grown in the ensuing years with inner-city unemployment at crisis levels. Opposing voices argued that the commission's prediction of separate societies had failed to materialize due to a marked increase in the number of African Americans living in suburbs.

The new report blames US policymakers and elected officials, saying they're not doing enough to heed the warning on deepening poverty and inequality that was highlighted by the Kerner Commission five decades ago, and it lists areas where the country has seen "a lack of or reversal of progress."

"Racial and ethnic inequality is growing worse. We're re-segregating our housing and schools again," stated former Democratic US Senator Fred Harris of Oklahoma, a coeditor of the new report and the last surviving member of the original Kerner Commission created by President Lyndon Johnson in 1967. "There are far more people who are poor now than was true fifty years ago. Inequality of income is worse."

The new study titled "Healing Our Divided Society: Investing in America Fifty Years After the Kerner Report" says the percentage of people living in deep poverty—less than half of the federal poverty level—has increased since 1975. About 46 percent of people living in poverty in 2016 were classified as living in deep poverty—sixteen percentage points higher than in 1975.

The new report calls on the federal government and states to push for more spending on early childhood education and a fifteen dollar national minimum wage by 2024. It also demands more regulatory oversight over lenders to prevent predatory lending, community policing that works with nonprofits in minority neighborhoods, and more job-training programs in an era of automation and emerging technologies.

Unlike the 1968 findings, the new report includes input from African Americans, Latinos, Native Americans, and women who are scholars and offer their own recommendations.

After reviewing the reports, I thought to myself, Have we as a society and nation digressed? Does history repeat itself? Have we become a callous people? Do we even care? Why are there so many similarities between then and now?

On Views of Race and Inequality, Blacks and Whites Are Worlds Apart— Pew Research Center

—ɯ—

About four in ten blacks are doubtful that the US will ever achieve racial equality.

Almost eight years after Barack Obama's election as the nation's first black president—an event that engendered a sense of optimism among many Americans about the future of race relations—a series of flashpoints around the US has exposed deep racial divides and reignited a national conversation about race. A new Pew Research Center survey finds profound differences between black and white adults in their views on racial discrimination, barriers to black progress, and the prospects for change. Blacks, far more than whites, say black people are treated unfairly across different realms of life, from dealing with the police to applying for a loan or mortgage. And for many blacks, racial equality remains an elusive goal.

An overwhelming majority of blacks (88 percent) say the country needs to continue making changes for blacks to have equal rights with whites, but 43 percent are skeptical that such changes will ever occur. An additional 42 percent of blacks believe that the country will eventually make the changes needed for blacks to have equal rights with whites, and just 8 percent say the country has already made the necessary changes.

A much lower share of whites (53 percent) say the country still has work to do for blacks to achieve equal rights with whites, and only 11 percent express doubt that these changes will come. Four in ten whites believe the country will eventually make the changes needed for blacks to have equal rights, and about the same share (38 percent) say enough changes have already been made.

These findings are based on a national survey by the Pew Research Center conducted February 29 to May 8, 2016, among 3,769 adults (including 1,799 whites, 1,004 blacks, and 654 Hispanics). The survey—and the analysis of the survey findings—is centered primarily around the divide between blacks and whites and on the treatment of black people in the US today. In recent years, this centuries-old divide has garnered renewed attention following the deaths of unarmed Black Americans during encounters with the police, as well as a racially motivated shooting that killed nine black parishioners at a church in Charleston, South Carolina, in 2015.

The survey finds that black and white adults have widely different perceptions about what life is like for blacks in the US. For example, by large margins, blacks are more likely than whites to say black people are treated less fairly in the workplace (a difference of forty-two percentage points), when applying for a loan or mortgage (forty-one points), in dealing with the police (thirty-four points), in the courts (thirty-two points), in stores or restaurants (twenty-eight points), and when voting in elections (twenty-three points). By a margin of at least twenty percentage points, blacks are also more likely than whites to say racial discrimination (70 percent vs. 36 percent), lower-quality schools (75 percent vs. 53 percent), and lack of jobs (66 percent vs. 45 percent) are major reasons that blacks may have a harder time getting ahead than whites.

More broadly, blacks and whites offer different perspectives of the current state of race relations in the US. White Americans are evenly divided, with 46 percent saying race relations are generally good, and 45 percent saying they are generally bad. In contrast, by a nearly two-to-one margin, blacks are more likely to say race relations are bad (61 percent) rather than good (34 percent). Blacks are also about twice as likely as whites to say too little attention is paid to race and racial issues in the US these days (58 percent vs. 27 percent). About four in ten whites (41 percent), compared with 22 percent of blacks, say there is too much focus on race and racial issues.

Blacks and whites also differ in their opinions about the best approach for improving race relations. Among whites, more than twice as many say that in order to improve race relations, it's more important to focus on what different racial and ethnic groups have in common (57 percent) as say the focus should be on what makes each group unique (26 percent). Among blacks, similar shares say the focus should be on commonalities (45 percent) as say it should be on differences (44 percent).

A Brief Historical Reflection of Race and Racism in the US Army

—⠶⠶—

Truth be told, I am a soldier—a soldier for life. Many would not understand, and perhaps some may even be critical of those who opted to serve. The military is a subculture within a culture. The military is a fraternity. The military exemplifies esprit de corps. After finishing a career outside of the military establishment, I can say with certainty that serving in the military was the closet I have ever come to experiencing true racial equality during my lifetime. Yet it had and still has its issues regarding race and racism. Still, I and many others before and after me served proudly.

While race and racism were prevalent throughout the history of our armed forces, I have chosen to briefly focus on the WWII era. WWII is considered the gateway to the modern-day, integrated, and all-volunteer military. During WWII, thousands of African American troops were sent to a defeated Germany to promote democracy, even as they had to deal with the realities of Jim Crow practices within the military. During that time, many posed the question, "How can America talk about German racism as long as it maintained separate white and black armies?" And the answer: America's function under Jim Crow and the military was no different.

It didn't matter that African American men had been essential to winning the war. A famed truck convoy called the Red Ball Express, made up of mostly black drivers, became invaluable to Gen. George S. Patton, delivering vital goods to allied troops on the front lines in France. The all-black 761st Tank Battalion fought valiantly in the Battle of the Bulge. The famed Tuskegee airmen escorted US bombers in Europe, engaging in air combat over Sicily, Italy, and Germany.

The occupation years, 1945–1955, would expose a glaring hypocrisy perpetuated by the United States. Black occupation troops were part of the effort to prevent the resurgence of Nazism, yet for years were housed in segregated quarters, barred from officers' clubs regardless of their rank, and openly slurred, harassed, and physically attacked by White American service members.

Discrimination toward black troops came not just from white soldiers but also the upper echelons of military leadership, including commanders who expressed their resentment of black service members for being a part of the occupation, bitter that blacks were allowed to represent America during the occupation. This behavior and conduct served to reinforce the military's racial hierarchy and maintain the perception that Jim Crow laws remained in effect, even overseas.

While these discriminatory practices were encountered within the military, there were locals who clung to Nazi views on white supremacy; however, Germans largely embraced black culture.

The indignities were well documented and used by the Soviet Union as a propaganda point during the early years of the Cold War. How could the United States promote free elections in Germany while it was mistreating its own citizens there and making it harder for them to vote at home? How ironic, even our enemies understood our hypocrisy.

On July 26, 1948, President Eisenhower signed Executive Order 9981, desegregating the entire armed forces. It declared, "There shall be equality of treatment and opportunity for all persons in the armed services without regard to race, color, religion, or national origin." The order was met with resistance, and it was not until 1954 that the military was actually integrated.

Present day, the chairman of the joint chiefs of staff, America's top uniformed officer, recently addressed racial equality within the armed forces, saying, "Our military has a mixed record on equality. While the military sets an example for civil society through our inclusiveness, we, too, have not come far enough. We all need to do better. For example, although the United States military has a higher proportion of African Americans serving in our ranks than in society at large, only 7 percent of our flag and general officers are African American."

For many African Americans, our reasons for serving were the same as others. Pride for one's country, a call to serve, family lineage, heraldry, and escape from poverty, education, and seeking better job opportunities are some of the primary reasons for serving. Historically, African Americans have used the military as a way to prove our worthiness of citizenship and to open up the doors to opportunity and possibility. This service continued despite unfair treatment. We vowed to be the best we could be.

References and Credits

- American Community Survey (a.k.a. ACS)
- "Beyond the World War II We Knew—After Fighting Nazis, Black G.I.s Faced Racism in U.S. Military" by Alexis Clark
- *More Than Equals: Racial Healing for the Sake of the Gospel*, Chris Rice, coauthor
- Drug Policy Alliance
- #Hypocrite#fake#two-faced#jive#lingo
- ervin062.web.unc.edu/reactions-to-civil-rights/using-religion-to-pose-and-defend-an-argument/
- extenze.com
- FBI 2012 "Supplementary Homicide Report"
- History.house.gov/Exhibitions-and-Publications/Civil-Rights/Civil-Rights/
- Education.findlaw.com/higher-education/affirmative-action-and-college-admissions.html
- Pew Research Center
- *The Guardian*
- *The Sentencing Project*
- United States Department of Labor
- US Bureau of Labor Statistics
- Vox's Dara Lind
- Www.Bourncreative.com/meaning-of-the-color-black/
- Www.Bourncreative.com/meaning-of-the-color-white/

- Www.RmgR.co.uk/sites/default/files/styles/rmg_landscape_medium/public/Slave percent20ship.jpg?itok=XIfC8EW0
- Www.Brennancenter.org/analysis/7-things-know-about-redistricting
- Www.Gotquestions.org/racism-Bible.html
- Www.Washingtonpost.com/local/hate-groups-in-the-us-remain-on-the-rise-according-to-new-study/2018/02/21/6d28cbe0-1695-11e8-8b08-027a6ccb38eb_story.html?utm_term=.f2c774648ada
- Www.Washingtonpost.com/posteverything/wp/2015/08/17/blacks-own-just-10-u-s-television-stations-heres-why/?utm_term=.ad64e3d7a0b1
- Www.Forbes.com/sites/robertpearl/2015/03/05/healthcare-black-latino-poor/#46549ec97869
- www.Nytimes.com/2018/11/13/us/hate-crimes-fbi-2017.html
- Young Invincibles
- Www.Floridamemory.com/Items/show/25883

About the Author

—ɷ—

After writing about professionalism in the workplace and the challenges of raising daughters, C. E. Dickens is proud to release his new publication, *It's As Plain As Black and White: (How Race and Racism Shaped and Motivated Me*. As a result of his lifelong endeavors, the author has shifted his focus to issues that he has a passion for, are purpose-driven, and can hopefully impact the lives of others in a positive way.

Being a son of the rural deep South, growing up in an impoverished neighborhood, being raised by a single mother, and having to overcome everyday challenges to be accepted and treated as an equal afforded the author a unique perspective on race and racism. C. E. Dickens was determined and motivated to rise above the negative stereotypes typically associated with his ethnicity.

The author is passionate about the realities of race and racism because he has:

- Experienced it
- Felt it
- Been affected by it
- Seen it
- Discussed it
- Opposed it
- Studied it
- Enforced policies and procedures about it
- Tried to understand it
- Triumphed over it

Made in the USA
Monee, IL
08 December 2020